LOVE,
CURIOSITY,
FRECKLES
AND DOUBT

Also by Pat Phoenix
ALL MY BURNING BRIDGES

LOVE, CURIOSITY, FRECKLES AND DOUBT

Pat Phoenix

Arlington Books
Clifford Street Mayfair
London

LOVE, CURIOSITY, FRECKLES AND DOUBT
First published September 1983 by
Arlington Books (Publishers) Ltd
3 Clifford Street Mayfair
London W1

Reprinted October 1983

© Pat Phoenix 1983

Typeset by Inforum Ltd, Portsmouth
Printed and bound by The Pitman Press Ltd, Bath

British Library Cataloguing in Publication Data
Phoenix, Pat
Love, curiosity, freckles and doubt.
1. Phoenix, Pat   2. Actors—Great Britain
—Biography
I. Title
791.45'028'0924   PN2598.P/

ISBN 0 85140 623 8

Illustrations

my fake fur coat. The newspapers later described it as "opulent fur". I ask you!

Tony's an avid Liverpool Football Club supporter and he couldn't resist this opportunity to kiss the League Championship trophy after the club won in the 81–82 season.

Summer seasons are lovely, and our show in Eastbourne in 1982 was no exception. We took time to do all the touristy things – walking on the prom, seeing the sights and soaking up the sun.

A surprise party for Tony's birthday last year (1982), and all our friends joined in the celebrations. I bought him an exercise bicycle which Chris Quentin, Tom Pendry, MP for Stalybridge and Hyde, Tony, Ernst Walder and Peter Dudley made me try for size.

Between pages 128 and 129

The day the Queen came down our *Street*. She's pictured here with Sir Denis Forman, Chairman of Granada, during her visit to the new set in 1982.

Exercise for Tony – and a little gentle sketching for me. A rare day off spent in the quiet of the conservatory at my cottage.

Tony and I share a love of music, and in our rare quiet moments we gather round the piano at the cottage for a good singsong.

Midnight . . . and another New Year begins. That's me in party mood at my cottage.

The side of things *Coronation Street* viewers don't see. With all those cameras, cables and overhead microphones crammed into the studio set of the Rovers, it's surprising there's any room left for the actors!

"Win the race, and I'll marry you," I told my racehorse, Lymond, at Thirsk in spring '83. Me and my big mouth . . . he won it, of course!

A pint in the Rovers for Dustin Hoffman when he visited the *Coronation Street* set in 1983. A super guy – Elsie and I both fell for him.

I love collecting paintings, and every one of them has a story to tell. There's hardly a spare inch of wall space in my cottage.

Good reason to celebrate. With all the changes that have taken place on *Coronation Street*, there are still a few old familiar faces left. Bill Roache, Doris Speed, Jack Howarth and me in the Rovers earlier this year (1983).

Tony and I with Dr Fred Pestalozzi and his English wife, Sylvia, in their garden overlooking Lake Zurich – a picture taken during our visit to the Bio-Strath laboratories in Switzerland in spring '83.

Relaxing at my health club.

Glamour girl – what me? The soft lighting at my health club does wonders for a woman.

Four be the things I am wiser to know;
Idleness, sorrow, a friend and a foe.

Four be the things I'd been better without;
Love, curiosity, freckles and doubt.

Three be the things I shall never attain;
Envy, content and sufficient champagne.

Three be the things I shall have till I die;
Laughter and hope and a sock in the eye.

Inventory by Dorothy Parker.
From *The Collected Poems of Dorothy Parker*,
published by Gerald Duckworth Limited.

Part One

Chapter One

"You devious bitch, you."

I laughed. "Of all the things you could call me, devious is not one of them."

For a moment his face cleared. I felt I had averted the storm. "True," he said and he almost smiled. "You could never be that." I saw the shadow cross his face again. "I'm sick of playing retainer to your Royal Highness. Your Royal Highness, the Queen of Nothing and Nowhere," he sneered.

I could feel tears sting behind my eyes. "Please," I begged, "don't let's have another screaming match. There are people in the other room—"

"People," he screamed, "always people. You're surrounded by bloody people."

The glass he'd been holding suddenly, unexpectedly, hit the wall an inch away from my head. Liquid splashed over my face and hands, fragments of glass showering over my hair and my shoulders. We stared at one another. Startled faces crowded the door. "What on earth was that crash?"

He was shrugging into his coat. "Ask her," he said. "Ask the Queen of bloody Nowhere."

The door slammed and he was gone.

A scene from a play? An extract from Virginia Woolf? No. Just a quick flash of what was becoming part of the daily routine of my second marriage.

How we got to that time of screaming and barely controlled violence after all the rosy dreams of the future, leaves me shaking my head in bewilderment, even now. Shaking my head and gasping for breath like someone drowning. How was I to know that those long, intimate evenings when, sprawled across cushions and warmed by firelight, we talked of art and religion, life and work, would turn into a nightmare, a dialogue of abuse? That the home I had worked to fill with softness and warmth would become a place to which I wished never to return? How was I to know that the kindly, gentle man I had married was to be so changed? That I was also to change?

Laughter died, love got lost and Alan Browning suffered so tragically. I suppose I have tried a hundred times to write the truth of what happened, wishing to hurt no one. But each time I tried, dressing up the words, pulling the punches, sentences stared back from the page like accusations.

There is only one way to tell it, and that's straight, regardless of what the world thinks. My real friends know the story and my enemies will say what they will, as they always have.

My wedding day was a good indication of what was to follow. I was running a temperature, coughing my heart out. My back ached and my chest hurt. My face still had a few angry weals across it.

Alan and I had had to play a violent row scene in the Street the day before, all part of the script. He was to hit me hard.

"Don't do it until the actual take," I said. "We want it to look real and the only way to do that is to actually hit me."

Alan was reluctant to do it.

Throughout the day we played half a dozen brittle row scenes, then came the moment of truth. Alan hit me so hard I went hurtling across the set, grabbing a chair to prevent myself from smacking into the wall. It was the last scene of the day and brought gasps from the cameramen and technicians. "Cut!" the floor manager yelled. "That was great. I won't ask you to do it again. We've got what we need and it was terrific."

I threw my arms around Alan's neck. "Great, darling."

"But your face," he said, "look at your face." The livid weals showed through my make-up. "Oh baby, it wasn't meant to be that hard."

"It'll look great on screen," I said. "And that's all that matters."

He kissed me. "It'll look lovely tomorrow," he said ironically, "walking down the aisle with ruddy great fingermarks across your face. They'll think I'm a wife beater."

It was to be a quiet wedding – the day before Christmas Eve – in the small village church up on the hill. But it wasn't. There were hundreds of people, fans and pressmen, crowding round the church. And I nearly didn't make it on time, because of my dress: it was beautiful, almost a period costume in rich purple velvet, made specially for me by a theatrical costumier. I have worn it since in several period plays. But on that day it did cause some problems. It was so heavy – it weighed eighty pounds – that I needed help to get into it. My bridesmaids were all so busy tarting themselves up that they forgot about me. It finished up with my friend Harry Shelton hooking me into my wedding dress.

The church was packed and there were people jostling outside. After the service we had to run the gauntlet in a vintage open Rolls Royce. And it was so cold up on the hill there. Even my heavy cape couldn't keep out the bitter wind.

The reception over, Alan and I returned home to the cottage, thinking it the best place to stay, quiet without masses of reporters following us. That evening I collapsed with lung congestion and that was how my honeymoon was spent.

The marriage was ill-fated from the start. But for a time – about six months, I think – we were happy.

Alan always thought I should be doing much more work in the theatre, away from the Street. First he wanted me to do a one-woman show, an idea I wasn't keen on. I like to share, and part of the fun of the theatre is the team work; building up something enormous together. Alan was persistent. "You're too good an actress to be wasting yourself in *Coronation Street*. You should be in the theatre, doing something prestigious," he would say.

Then one day we received a letter from a friend of mine, Bill Kenmore, suggesting that we consider doing a tour of New Zealand. "The people out there are wonderful and they'll love you," he wrote. It was the ideal opportunity. We married in December 1972 and a year later we left *Coronation Street* and started to tour Britain. We must have played almost every theatre in the country – and usually to packed houses, I'm glad to say. Then we set off for a three-and-a-half-month tour of New Zealand with the play *Gaslight*.

We were happy and life was full of hope and adventure. But even then Alan's drinking was far advanced. I didn't learn until much later that even before our marriage he was drinking two bottles of gin a day. At that time I didn't connect drink with being ill. The idea of alcoholism had never occurred to me.

Of course, I knew he drank. To cope with the pressures of our profession, as with journalists, artists and people in many other careers, many actors drink. It's called social drinking. People meet at the end of a hard day's work to chat and wind down. In some professions the bar or the club is where much of the day's work is done. Business contacts are established, information exchanged, deals sealed. But all this doesn't mean to say these people are drunks – or alcoholics for that matter.

When I first knew Alan he was very much a man's man. You know the sort of thing: drinks with the boys, games of snooker, the lads' night out. He could drink heartily all night without seemingly coming to a state of drunkenness or being physically harmed in any way. He told me once that he had been in 'the wilderness' for a while. That he had been drinking heavily but had come out of it. Neither of us realised then that he would return to, and eventually die alone in, that wilderness.

While we were on tour Alan's drinking became more apparent, and what started as headaches and slight pain was later to manifest as something much worse. There were terrible rows. Perhaps for a day we could go without an argument – but no longer than that. It is so difficult to say what started them. The slightest thing could set one off.

On tour it is usual for the company to meet at the pub on pay day for a drink and a chat. A chance to get together and talk through any problems the cast might be having with the performance. But Alan would rather go home with a bottle of gin and get slowly drunk by himself.

"Come on, let's go and have a drink with the company," I urged on one occasion.

"Sod the company," Alan said. "You're surrounded by people all the time."

The truth was that I was beginning to dread being alone with him. It was getting to the point where, when we were alone, he would either pick a fight or drink himself senseless.

On another occasion we were playing at a theatre three miles or less from home. Driving back after the evening performance, Alan got lost and we didn't arrive home until the early hours of the morning.

"For God's sake, Alan," I said. "Couldn't you have stopped the car and asked someone?"

But, of course, he daren't stop the car. He was drunk. It didn't occur to me then that he couldn't risk breathing on anybody.

We were in bed, me with a pot of tea at my bedside, he with a glass of gin at his. He turned to me, his face black with temper, and flung the contents of the glass at me.

"You bastard . . . " I spluttered.

Alan shrugged down into the bed. Now normally I'm a very feeling person and if I'm going to throw a teapot I test the temperature first. This time I didn't. I took off the lid and tipped the hot tea all over him. He was so drunk he didn't feel a thing. He had teabags all over his head and behind his ears. He woke up the next morning like that with not a clue of where they'd come from.

Occasionally I tried to appeal to him: "Don't you think you ought to cut down?" or "Please, Alan, not another drink." I wasn't nagging. I thought it was for his own good, especially as he seemed to be in more and more pain after each drinking bout. But he only flew into a rage, which made it impossible to broach the subject too frequently. I found myself recoiling from his anger and began to withdraw.

All this was kept very much from the public. He was never obviously drunk or incapable of performing. There was only one occasion when he went on stage and changed the whole of the performance. The character he played became something else again. It was only when I took a close look at his eyes and saw that they were totally bloodshot that I realised he had been drinking.

Life was becoming more difficult – for both of us. I played every scene I knew to get him to pull back on his drinking – begging, pleading, cajoling – losing my laughter in the process. I was wasting my time; it was already too late.

One day, on his way between the lounge and kitchen carrying his usual silver goblet – "Orange juice, darling, just orange juice" – he slipped and fell, the goblet lodged under his ribs. He was in terrible pain and, in panic, I sent for the doctor. He examined Alan carefully, his face grave. Whitefaced I waited, dreading what was to come. The doctor looked first at me and then back to Alan.

"If you don't stop drinking now, you'll be dead in three months," he said. He told Alan in detail how he would die if he didn't stop. "Alcoholics often choke in their own blood . . ." Then he turned to me and said: "You'll have just three minutes to get to me when it happens." But, sadly, when it did, I wasn't there.

For a time I thought Alan was going to stop drinking. I think he did try. I'm sure he tried. But it was all too much for him. After a short time he seemed to become ill again and I found out, only by accident, that he was deceiving me. That he was lacing his orange juice with gin and vodka. The rows became fast and furious. It became a regular thing for Alan to manufacture an argument and bang out of the house.

"I won't come back," he'd say. "Never, ever."

But I knew that he would. I knew he would come home, after a heavy drinking session, battered, bruised and looking more ill than ever.

Finally, after a tremendous row, when he was packing up and walking out, I begged him for his own sake not to do so. "If you go this time," I said, "it'll be for keeps." He left.

I didn't hear anything for some time. Then one day, out of the blue, his agent rang me. "It's Alan. He's very ill," she said.

I discovered that he had locked himself in a flat in London and collapsed. I panicked once more. I tried everyone and everything to help him. I tried the Samaritans, a private ambulance, Alcoholics Anonymous . . . everything. But I was in Manchester and Alan was in London. The situation seemed impossible.

Finally I got in touch with one of his friends. Barry went to the flat and kicked down the door to get to Alan. But Alan refused to go to hospital.

"All right, old boy. Let's go for a drink instead," Barry said.

It was the only way he could get Alan to move. He kidded him that they were going to the pub and drove him to the hospital.

Back on his feet, Alan came out of hospital and we tried once more. All this time, as far as the public and the press were concerned, we were leading an apparently happy life. But there had been other separations. Before the tour of New Zealand, literally months after we had married, we had a terrible blow-up and Alan returned to London. We had contracted to do the tour, Alan and me together, and there we were separated.

Realising the situation, my boss at the time said: "Look, Pat, if it's going to be terribly difficult for you we could bring in another actor to replace Alan."

"I don't want to," I said.

"But, if it's going to be difficult—"

"No, no, please. He'll be all right. Maybe in some way we can try and work out our differences."

So Alan came back. It was a sort of truce. But I told him I would not live with him as his wife until he pulled himself together. We went off on tour quite happily. But when we got there he started a row about billing because my name, as leading lady, was in top place. We had separate suites, too. Both of them were nice but Alan thought mine was better than his.

"Bloody star," he shouted. The rest of the company and the hotel staff turned and stared.

"Alan, please," I said. "Not here—"

"Bloody star, you have to have everything your own way."

In actual fact, it was nothing to do with me. The suites and rooms were allocated by the management. But Alan caused an absolute uproar and for the sake of everybody, the company and the management, I said he could move in with me. So we tried once more to make a go of it. That must have lasted about three weeks and then he was off on the bottle once more.

Towards the end, when we had split up yet again, the press found out. I couldn't give Alan away. He was then still able to work and I would never harm his career. So, when asked by the press the reason for the split, I said I was inadequate. What the hell, I'd always thought so anyway. I left them to find out what I meant. Inadequate? Well, inadequate to stop the rot, to stop Alan drinking, to save him in any way. One day we could be as happy as Larry and that would probably be the day Alan would try to cut back on his booze. But he couldn't for long. The next day he would be sodden again and I couldn't come in the door without something hurtling past my ear.

Amongst all the bitterness, I have some gentle, soft memories of Alan. He would lie at the top of the stairs, face to face with the dogs, talking to them. He could be lovely, sensitively recreating for me the moments of his past life which he cherished, things he loved.

But most of the time it was tearing me apart, watching this lovely man changing before my very eyes. Imagine marrying a man who said he loved you and showed all the signs of loving you. And on alternative days behaving as though he wished you were dead. Can you imagine living like that? That was my life for about five years, until we finally separated. I was doing a double act and driving myself crazy. There I was trying to maintain the cool exterior while, inside, I was a veritable volcano of emotion. In a strange way I felt somehow guilty, responsible for not being able to stop this rot.

Physical relations stopped. They had to. I had in effect been going to bed with someone who wasn't the man I married. My life has to be as honest as I can possibly make it. I even find it difficult to keep secrets. I'm totally open about everything I do because I'm not clever enough to be anything other than that. With Alan I couldn't win either way. There was only one thing to do, I thought. Get out. Get out so that I wouldn't have to sit there and watch him die.

Chapter Two

So that was it. The finale. We had separated for the last time.

I'm not saying it was all Alan's fault. Of course it wasn't. Alcoholism is a sickness. But on the other hand, I'm not the easiest person in the world to live with. I had to work and keep on working. I had to be away from Alan every day and he couldn't stand that. But somehow, though we were legally separated, I still felt responsible. I kept in touch. Every time I heard that Alan was ill I would ring his agent or she would ring me either to say that he wanted to see me, or, even, to ask whether I knew where he was.

I remember one time I was determined to go to see Alan who was once more in hospital. My friend Peter Dudley kindly offered to drive me. It was a hell of a journey for both of us. I was working all day and it was a mad dash to get there on time. We arrived to see Alan lying ashen-faced on an austere hospital bed, his body full of tubes leading in every direction.

"Hello darling," I said. "It's good to see you."

He smiled and even held out an arm, which was about all he could move. "Glad you came," he said.

As I walked out of the room to talk to the doctor, Alan turned to Peter and I heard him say, "That bitch will say it's because of the drink."

The change, you see, was instantaneous. One moment glad to see me, the next accusing.

"That bitch will say it's because of the drink," he said. Which of course it was. As I came back into the room he said: "Hello darling. How lovely to see you."

The hypocrisy was horrific. But I knew it wasn't really Alan talking. Later, there were nightmare pictures in the papers and stories of his drunken behaviour, being arrested and appearing in court. Half of it I didn't know about then, thank God. Tales came to me afterwards.

By September of that last year, 1979, I was desperate for a holiday.

"Let's get away," I said to the gang – Peter Dudley, Ernst Walder, my housekeeper Kitty, Nell, Carole and the rest of my friends. "We'll take a cottage somewhere in Cornwall and just disappear for a while."

The house we stayed in had no phone. It was beautiful. So quiet. But we had only been there a couple of days, had barely unpacked, when the next-door neighbour called by.

"There's a telephone call for you, Miss Phoenix. It's Granada Television," she said.

I must add that I never go anywhere without first telling Granada where I'm going. You never know. There might be some emergency which means I'm needed back on the Street. So my boss knew where I was and had managed to reach me.

"Alan's very ill," said the voice on the telephone.

"Is he . . . is he . . . ?" I couldn't get the words out.

"No. He's all right at the moment but he is seriously ill and we thought you ought to know."

"Should I come back?" I said. "Would it help?"

"Well, it is up to you, of course. But I would suggest you don't come back just yet. The hospital is surrounded by reporters and they're only waiting for you to walk in," she said.

I returned to the cottage. "It's about Alan," I told the others, "he's very ill." There were doubtful looks from Kitty and Nell who'd heard it all before.

"It could be that he's crying wolf," I added, "but it doesn't sound like it."

"You can't do anything," said Peter. "You can't do anything now and it would do no good to go back. Stay here. You'll hear if he gets any worse."

There had been so many calls before saying he was dying. So many attempts to get me to his side. Certainly not because he loved me, I thought. Possibly he needed me at that time.

Indecision. What should I do? Should I go back and tell Alan a lot of lies to get him better? Tell him we would get back together and all would be lovely? Supposing he recovered? I couldn't have gone through all that again. So . . . I stayed away. I think I was suffering from an over-fevered imagination. I could see him lying there, dying alone, and yet I couldn't go. I felt the only way I could survive was to stay away because it was killing me too.

"Come out to dinner," Peter said, "and put it out of your mind."

Ernst hadn't joined us at this time but was due to arrive from Yorkshire later. The rest of us went out to my old mate Roland Morris's place, the Admiral Benbow in Penzance. We had a great dinner. We talked and laughed about the old days when we had all been terribly happy together before I'd married. Late that night we returned to the cottage. As we drove towards it I could see two strange cars parked outside. Peter helped me out of the car and Ernst came towards me. He kissed me and whispered, softly: "It's the press. Be very careful what you say."

A reporter stepped out of the shadows. "We'd like your reactions to Mr Browning's death," he said.

I think I must have visibly fallen back on to Peter's arm.

"But, I've been in touch with everybody . . . this afternoon," I said. "Nobody said . . . They said he was getting better. He's not . . . I don't believe he's dead."

The photographer put his hand on Peter's arm and drew him away from me. "Could we," he said, "have a picture of you with your arm around Miss Phoenix, consoling her in her grief?"

The words Peter used to that man are unprintable. We all moved inside the house and slammed the door. Alone, later, I cried with grief for the waste of a life, for Alan himself and for his children.

It is a well-recorded fact that at times of tragedy people laugh. It's a sort of hysteria we all have within us. I got the giggles three days later over the way the press were hounding us. They pursued us all over Cornwall, changing cars. It was like a detective movie. There was no way we could shake them off.

In the end I turned to Peter and said: "There is no way we are going to lose them. The only thing to do is to lead the reporters to a place we want to go to."

We drove to a quiet little Cornish church. Peter, Ernst and I went inside and sat down. I heard footsteps behind us. As I turned I saw one of the reporters. Suddenly I felt a rush of anger.

"What is it you want?" I said. "What are you creeping about for?"

He whispered: "Could we see you outside, Miss Phoenix?"

"What?" I demanded. "Are you afraid to speak in the presence of God?" I really meant that.

"No, no. It's not quite that . . . " Eventually he persuaded us to go outside. The usual questions. How did I feel? How long had my friends been with me? Then, I must say, he behaved in a much politer way than other reporters had done before.

We went back home, although we hadn't shaken them off entirely. There were other freelance reporters banging on the door and giving us no peace. We saw the newspapers the next day. The photograph of the three of us, taken outside the church was there – under headlines 'Plot to kill the Pope'. It made us look like hit men. Again we got the giggles.

I was distraught and yet in a strange way relieved. I was free. But to have my freedom that way was terrible. I wasn't to know that the guilt and horror I felt at that time was to take more than a year to shake off.

I didn't go to the funeral. Alan's ex-wife and children were there and somehow I felt they had priority. I sent a wreath. "Another time, another place. Tricia." People are still asking me what it meant.

In the Street Elsie Tanner had separated from Alan Howard. He wrote to her saying he had met another woman and wanted a divorce. Granada had asked Alan Browning in to do the voice-over while I was away.

It was at the time that we had separated, too, for the last time. I didn't hear his voice until the actual take which was several months before he died. As Elsie was reading the letter, Alan's voice came over the sound system. His voice had gone. It was gin-soaked, almost unrecognisable. I knew then that he was dying.

Elsie was supposed to cry, but not as much as Pat cried. I broke down completely.

"Cut," called the floor manager. I couldn't stop weeping.

After Alan's death I lived a sort of twilight existence. I lost my self-confidence, my capacity to love and, most important of all, my sense of humour. How at my age could I start to live again? And, besides, I didn't feel I wanted to. I didn't want another man in my life. I felt I'd had too much of a bumpy ride already. Having had two marriages fall apart, I finally came to the decision that marriage was simply not for me. Obviously, I thought, I was one of those people who were unable to make it work.

I remember Violet Carson telling me: "You see. I told you so. You're not the marrying kind. I know what you're like when they take your freedom away. Fratchin' to get out, that's you all the time." Well, it wasn't what split Alan and me up but maybe she was right in some ways. Having been told that by so many people, I had begun to believe it. Perhaps they were right. Perhaps I wasn't the marrying kind. There were suitors. The odd casual dinner. But I had no interest.

There is something sad about the solitary life. People who live alone, and like it. But I am not one of those. I am a sharer. I like to share everything. There I was beginning to behave like the complete spinster. I buried myself under as much work as I could possibly do.

But my mind kept harping back. I kept thinking of the nice, gentle man I had loved and married. Of the fun we'd had together before drink ruined his life. His gentleness then was surprising in such a big man. He seemed to understand the emotions of others, their small aches and pains – and the big ones too. He was a dreamer, a poet who wooed me with flowers and regaled me with stories.

I remember with warmth the time we were looking for a house and found the cottage I still live in – that *Random Harvest*-type cottage everyone dreams of. *Random Harvest* was one of the plays in which Alan and I had a huge success when we were touring together. It is a beautiful love story, a real weepie. In the film of the play, the cottage where Paula and her lover set up home is so very pretty. Covered in rambling roses, with a little white wicket gate and a brook running in front. I fell in love with it immediately. My cottage has the white wicket gate and a creeper covering the walls. But – as I discovered later to my horror – the brook runs underneath!

To me the Random Harvest cottage was a symbol of happy endings. A cottage that wasn't too grand, and that was warm and cosy, even a little higgledy-piggledy. So when Alan and I decided to look for a home to start our new life together, it was my ideal. We came down the lane one winter's evening and saw the cottage. The windows were gleaming, the place looked warm and inviting. We walked inside and I gasped.

"This is it," I said. "This is absolutely it. *Random Harvest* all over again."

It has never quite matched the film image. The cottage is too tall and rambling. A different shape altogether. But many of my friends have found a Random Harvest haven here in their times of trouble. The top floor has been somewhere they could escape to.

After Alan's death the cottage was full of memories. Memories of things we had done together. Memories of the happy times and the unhappy times too. I felt I ought to get away. To sell, to wipe the slate clean and start again. But somehow the cottage wouldn't let me. It didn't want me to sell. It wanted me to stay. So I changed my mind and stayed. Me and the dogs, and Kitty and my usual friends who never deserted me for a single moment during that terribly bumpy period.

When Alan and I moved in, my dogs came with us. I love the dogs and Alan did too. He would sit for hours talking to them and playing. When, after our last separation, he had written articles in the *News of the World* about our life together, what he wrote about the dogs hurt me very much. Amongst other things, silly things, like saying I changed my clothes fifteen times a day – little snippets, slightly distorted, about myself and my friends, some of them completely in his imagination – he also said that I kept all the dogs with me on the bed. That wasn't true. I didn't. Alan did.

The more he drank the more he lost his sense of fun. In the early days holidays together were full of exploring. Looking at new places and finding new things to admire in nature. He seemed as involved and as interested as I was. After the first year, he became more and more disinclined to go out unless there was drinking involved. And plenty of booze at that. Even dinner-party invitations from my friends he sneered at. "I'm not going there. For one lousy bottle of plonk," he'd say. It was useless to suggest a drive or a walk on the moors. Alan would rather stay home and drink himself senseless. Most of our holidays after then were spent with me going to places with other people and Alan remaining in the hotel or the cottage drinking. Always when I returned he'd be in a towering rage at my having gone out.

Alan was a splendid actor. He had a splendid reputation. But towards the end there were times when his illness caused him to forget his lines, and on one occasion he fell to the studio floor. People were kind, saying how very ill he was. Polite parlance, perhaps, in our profession rather than saying how drunk he was. But sober he could be brilliant.

On the first night of our New Zealand tour of *Gaslight*, playing in Wellington, where every seat had been sold for months, Ivan Beavis who played Inspector Rough went down with food poisoning, suddenly, unexpectedly – and terrifyingly for all of us.

"Well," said Alan, "we have to go on. We've a house that's packed to capacity. If Rough isn't there, half the play is gone. You'll have to do it, girl. Nobody else can."

There was the usual excited murmuring in the audience before a first night curtain goes up. A drum roll and I timorously slipped through the curtain in costume. "Ladies and gentlemen," I said. "It is unfortunate tonight that we have lost our leading man due to a case of food poisoning. We are unable to perform *Gaslight* in its entirety."

A great moan of disappointment came from the audience.

"But we can offer you an alternative," I said. "We can play *Gaslight* to you in potted form. I will tell the story, the actors that remain will play it. And after that we'll have a party. If that meets with your approval perhaps you'll let me know. If not, your money will be returned at the box office."

There was a moment's silence and then a great roar of approval from the audience. Only two people left the theatre that night. We played what is known as a blinder. It was quite hysterical in some ways because I was automatically changing my voice to say the lines of Inspector Rough and even changing position on the stage. Doing it off the top of your head like that is not an easy thing to do. But we got through it.

"You played a marathon there, Pat," said Philip, our impresario. "You played a belter, I can tell you."

Judging by the applause, the audience loved it. We did the play and still had an hour to fill. So we changed, had an interval and did a party night. Alan played his guitar, I gave them some poetry. The whole company joined in with musical instruments. We went down into the audience and talked to people. It was quite a night. A night that will long be remembered in the annals of Wellington's theatre history. The next day the papers were filled with rave notices.

That was an exciting, brilliant night. But there were the other times. Terrible times which in retrospect seem almost funny. Like the time I got drunk in a vain attempt to make Alan stop for my sake. I tried time and time again to picture the agony of being permanently parched, permanently thirsty. Always needing that other drink. Was it like my needing another cigarette?

To try and understand I once drank him drink for drink in the hope that he would see what it was doing to me, and stop. It finished up with him being apparently sober and me being roaring drunk. So drunk I couldn't get up the stairs. I had to crawl up on my hands and knees. Suffice it to say, I was ill for four days after that.

I tried. I really did try to understand but never having been there, I couldn't. I only learned that people who are alcoholic

will lie, cheat and steal, and give away the dearest thing they
have for a drink.

Chapter Three

After the failure of my first marriage I had become afraid. I didn't particularly want to marry again. I saw no point; there was no question of children. But Alan, I think, saw that I was afraid. Afraid to make the total commitment. I felt I was letting him down in some way by refusing him. He started to become bad tempered and irritable, because, or so I thought then, he was old-fashioned and needed me to make that commitment. So I had to do it, didn't I? I suppose at the bottom of me I had the feeling that I shouldn't really do it. But I talked myself into it. Simply fear.

You're afraid of yourself more than anything else, I thought. I *was* afraid. Petrified. I was shaking in my shoes as I said, "I do." Not afraid of Alan but of myself. Would I feel myself tied again? Would I be able to cope with making decisions for two rather than one?

But fools rush in where angels fear to tread. And there was I, standing at the altar for the second time around. Even then I never really became Mrs Browning. I think that made him feel resentful. There were embarrassing moments when we went out. Well-meaning people would say the wrong thing. "Hello Miss Phoenix. How nice to see you. Is that Mr Browning with you?" Alan felt it was humiliating. It was lowering. He had a very old-fashioned attitude towards women.

The sequence of events in those years of marriage and

separation is still so confused in my mind even to this day. Things happened so suddenly. The days and nights ran into one. Nights when I got no sleep and days that I spent worrying about Alan's whereabouts. There was a time when I got to dread coming home, not knowing what to expect. The home that had been a haven became a nightclub – and I couldn't live in it.

Alan had special friends, I learned later, to whom he spoke about me disparagingly. He brought them home to stay for weeks. To eat and drink and then float off again. Drunks – and there you're talking about some of the famous. There are a lot of alcoholics in our business. Careers can – and often have been – ruined by drink. But his friends made me feel like a martinet when I begged them not to take Alan out drinking.

"Come on ol' lad, you're coming for a drink," they'd say. I'd get so angry when they dragged him out and sent him home paralytic. They refused to accept what they were doing to him. Then there would be scenes. "He is dying," I pleaded, "and you're murdering him. Go on pouring drink down him and he'll be dead. Don't you see that?" They thought I was being bitchy. They muttered at me. They took no notice and so, in a way, those closest to him helped him on his way.

For some, drinking is all part of the day's routine. But there is a fine line between social drinking and alcoholism. In those years Alan quietly crossed it. He crossed it when he started having gin with his morning orange juice. He crossed it when he put a bottle of booze and a paper cup in the car. And the more he drank, the more he changed. He began to find fault in me constantly. God knows, I'm not perfect, but surely not so full of fault as that. I hate rows. Life is short – and how most of us long for it to be sweet. I wanted what everyone else wants, I think. The beautiful things in life. And by that I mean not so much money but good relationships, warmth and friendship.

Alan's constant fault-finding finally convinced me that he

didn't love me. But when he was sober he did. Drunk, a totally different character took over. His mind switched completely from "Darling, I love you" to "you f . . . . . . bitch". A total Jekyll and Hyde performance. He would be calling me everything under the sun one minute, then someone would come in and it would be "my lovely wife". I couldn't stand it. It was hypocritical. It was foul. But in reality, only part of his disease.

About once a month he would go off to get sloshed and after about four days would ring me as if nothing had happened. Each time he did that I had to pick up my life again. I thought he meant it. One moment we were together, deciding to make a go of our marriage, the next I was on my own, having to learn to live again as a single person. And the moment after that, he would appear once more. Something dreadful was happening to me. I found it difficult to smile. When he was in the house it was as if a great weight was upon me. I became quieter and quieter. A stranger to my friends.

And so, for me, it was all over before Alan died. It finished the day the doctor told me he was going to die if he didn't stop drinking. And Alan didn't stop. I begged, pleaded, tried everything I could think of to persuade him to get help at least.

"I need no help," he snarled.

I couldn't bear it any more. At that point I truly loved him and I felt I couldn't sit there and watch him poison himself to death. No matter what he did to me, I still loved him.

I have the greatest pity for any woman, or man, who is married to an alcoholic. I know how their compassion takes them down too. Quite how far down I slipped, I don't think the world ever suspected. I hoped I was a good enough actress to hide my feelings. But in reality I was a sort of walking nervous breakdown. And yet, in a sense, I breathed easier after Alan's death. I knew there was going to be nothing to hurt me when I got home. Just as much as I knew there would be nothing to love me; I was in limbo.

I've always smoked too much. I began to smoke even more. I filled my life with activity, all of it superficial, public appearances – opening things, closing things. Anything and everything, but nothing with any depth. And then my friends stepped in.

"Stop it. Stop it now. It's time you really started to be you again," they said.

Two of them, Jim and Judy, used to fly us somewhere exciting every New Year. They made sure I was never left alone then. The first time, after Alan's death, we went to Maxim's in Paris. Jim rang to tell me the plan. "Oh, Jim," I said, "I'm working the day of New Year's Eve, and the day after too. It's a weekday."

"Don't worry," he said. "When you leave Granada that afternoon, there'll be a Rolls Royce waiting to take you to the airport. There you'll meet up with the others on the private plane. And when we land at Orly, there'll be limousines to take us to the hotel, the Georges Cinq. It's all arranged."

I remember the breathless excitement of that evening. We were like kids, all of us. We swept into Maxim's on a high of anticipation. Before us stood a Christmas tree covered in white orchids. There were flowers and feathers for the ladies. White straw hats for the fellas. The meal – oh, the meal was rapture and a wonder. The Dom Perignon flowed like water. We left as dawn broke over Paris, wishing Happy New Year to complete strangers. Arms around each other, we strolled down the boulevards to have coffee in some quaint street café. Then, back to the hotel to bathe and change before catching the plane home. Back at work that afternoon, I still hadn't come down from that wonderful evening.

There was a moment in Maxim's which set us all giggling. The waiter approached me. "Madam," he said. "There is a telephone call from a Meester Barry Manilow. Phoning you from Monte Carlo."

Peter stared at me. "And what the hell are you doing with Barry Manilow?" he said.

I was nuts then about Barry Manilow. I dashed from the table to the telephone. "Happy New Year, Pat," said the voice on the other end . . . the voice of my old friend Keith Pollitt. He thought the quickest way to get attention was to say he was Barry Manilow.

Keith is one of my true, true friends and he has seen me through most of my troubles. It was he who kept me going after Alan's death. He made me work, made me go out. He's a great optimist. A great forger ahead. He has the verve and vivacity of some American impresario. But he's not the burly six-footer you might expect. Keith is small, curly-haired and with a face like a cherub.

One morning when I was feeling particularly down, he arrived on the doorstep. "I've had an invitation," I said, "to go to Scotland. To Kirkcaldy, to friends there who have been wonderful."

He looked at me and said: "Well, I'm doing nothing for a couple of days. Why don't we go? Get your bag packed. We'll go."

It was a fine, fresh morning as we drove into Scotland. We drove along the bank of Loch Lomond, enjoying every minute of it. Stopping here and there just to look at the scenery. We arrived in Kirkcaldy towards evening. If you've never been there, I suggest you do, one day. The warmth of the people and their hospitality is overwhelming. They prepared rooms for us in their lovely hotel. White-carpeted suites, one each. The rooms were laden with every possible kind of drink you could wish to have.

Their concern for our comfort was a joy. Whenever I do raise a glass, I always drink a silent toast to my friends at Kirkcaldy. It was a wonderful weekend. We explored castles in fresh, pink-clouded mornings. We drove along the coast to small villages dotted with white cottages. People were gentle to me. I was out of the glare of publicity for a short time and we both loved every moment of it. There was one occasion when the hospitality became too much for me. People in their kindness were pressing drinks on me. I couldn't possibly cope with that large amount so I found myself passing my drink quietly to Keith or pouring it into the nearest plant pot.

And then it was time to go home. We meandered slowly over the hills. It was a rainy day and there was a rainbow.

"Let's find the end of the rainbow," I said.

"To find the crock of gold? Okay." Keith drove along a winding lane. Suddenly, we saw a signpost. 'Brig'o'doon', it said.

"So it really exists," said Keith. "I never knew."

"Neither did I. Let's get out of the car and explore," I said eagerly.

Ahead we saw this ridiculous, beautiful bridge. It was in fact the famous Tam o'Shanter's bridge mentioned in Burns's poem. Underneath nestled the tiny village of Brig'o'doon. Six or seven houses in the shadow of the bridge. Just then the rain stopped and the rainbow disappeared.

We had to travel on. "Let's call in at the Lake District on the way back," said Keith. We did that too. We stopped at a friend's cottage he knew. There again, more drinks, more hospitality.

Late that night we arrived home, me to the cottage and Keith to his home. Both of us with happy memories of a beautiful weekend. It was in moments like that, among close friends and the beauty of the countryside, when I started to come alive again. Keith and my friends and my working companions on the Street helped me greatly.

One night amidst all my gloom and doom, there came a knock on my door. It was Keith, Peter Dudley, Cheryl Murray and the rest of the gang.

"Come on, Pat. Get dressed, we're going out on the town," they said.

"No, not me," I said quietly. "You go on without me."

"You're coming," said Keith firmly.

That was that. I got changed and we all went off to a club in Manchester, the Golden Garter. Now I seldom go clubbing, but my friends were determined to cheer me up. Freddie Starr was appearing that night and they wanted me to see the show. We took our seats and Freddie Starr came on stage. Part way through his act, he spotted us in the audience.

"Eee, Elsie, what are you doing here?" he clowned.

We went backstage after the show and I was introduced to Freddie. He is a great guy and we hit it off straight away. We all left the Golden Garter very late to go back to Freddie's hotel. The hotel staff had stayed up for him and joined the rest of us in the lounge for a few drinks. We were talking about life and our particular problems, and Freddie was very understanding, trying to help wherever he could. The conversation became more philosophical and obviously very private.

Suddenly a couple walked across the lounge and butted rather rudely into the conversation.

"Elsie, it's good to see you. I said to my wife, I said, I'm sure that's Elsie Tanner over there . . ." They went on and on.

Poor Freddie was completely ignored and couldn't get a word in. Then the husband turned absent-mindedly to him.

"Don't I know you from somewhere?" he asked.

"A lot of people say he looks like Freddie Starr," I joked.

"Oh no," said the husband. "I know Freddie Starr. I've met 'im."

"Well, actually," I said, desperately trying to keep my face straight, "he's my son." I tapped my forehead knowingly, as if to indicate that the poor lad wasn't quite all there.

Freddie immediately launched into his act. "Ma, ma," he cried, sucking his thumb. He began rocking backwards and forwards in his chair. "Ma, ma." He fell off and rolled about on the floor. The rest of us tried hard to hide our laughter.

The couple looked at one another, shook their heads and walked off, saying, "Poor Elsie, I never knew."

It was an off-the-cuff performance – perhaps a little cruel but we all felt those people had been so rude to interrupt a private conversation in that way and then to ignore Freddie.

That night I felt I had met a kindred spirit. Freddie is a very sensitive, very understanding man, something which perhaps doesn't come over on stage. We talked the night away and he helped me considerably at a time when I was so far down. He will always be a good friend and, although he and his family are in one side of the country and I'm in the other, we try to keep in contact as much as possible.

In March 1976 – a little over three years after Alan and I were married – I returned to *Coronation Street*. By then Alan's drinking had caused us to separate once. We had finished touring and when Granada asked me back I accepted. It didn't look like Alan was going to work again and I had financial responsibilities. I wanted to work of course but it meant that I had to work even harder. I also had doubts, wondering if living together, eating together, sleeping together twenty-four hours a day was bad for us. I thought, if I worked apart from him it might ease the situation. Alan had vowed he would never return to the Street. And so when I was asked I went back. Gladly. It was, in a sense, a relief to get away. Also, returning to the Street was like coming home.

We often say in *Coronation Street* that being together for so long we are more married than married. We understand, perhaps, each other's pains and problems a little better. Our own stupidities, our faults and failings. We understand each other's moments of embarrassment, the lack of privacy and the good in all of us. The in-jokes which no one else could possibly share. Our long-running joke is that only *Coronation*

Street is the reality. Outside is make-believe. There was also the wit who started off the catchphrase, 'Goodbye, real world.' On filming days the studio rings with that cry.

There were those, of course, who shook their heads at me and said: "I told you it wouldn't work." There were others who stood by me regardless. And then there was my own philosophy – that you have to take a chance in life. If you don't take chances, you never do anything.

Fans, too, gave me tremendous support. Only a matter of days after Alan's death I had to do a public appearance in Cornwall. My great friend Charles Neave-Hill, then Master of Land's End, had asked me some time before and I had promised to go. But on the day I was nervous and still shattered by Alan's death. "I'm a bit afraid," I told Peter Dudley and Ernst Walder who were with me. "What are the people going to think after the newspaper reports?" (The press, you'll remember, were still hounding me for my reaction to Alan's death.)

"You? Afraid? Don't be silly," Ernst said.

"The public are fond of you," Peter told me. "They're not as daft as some people might think."

So sticking my chin out, with head high, I went. I'd hardly set foot in the place before the crowd was surging around me and people were throwing their arms around my shoulder.

"You'll be better now, love," one kindly, motherly woman said. "Don't worry about what they say in the papers. We don't believe that rubbish."

Hundreds of people, from all over Britain were surrounding me and giving me the most tremendous support. The way they dismissed all the stories for what they were worth was wonderful. Remember, I'm playing a woman who's no better than she should be, with an obvious north country accent and what is termed in our part of the country as 'no edge'. One grey-haired, well-dressed lady came up to me and said: "Don't be silly. We know you, you're our Pat. We wouldn't think such things about you." I felt humbled and extremely grateful for such kindness and warmth.

This came to mind again last Christmas when the vicar of a small parish in Salford asked me to open the church jumble sale. The area is very rundown. They're pulling down the houses all around and most of the people are unemployed. When I got to the hall it was full of people. I was feeling ill, I had lung congestion again and my back was hurting. But I tried to sparkle. I hesitated at the doorway. Now, remember, Pat, I told myself. Sparkle, sparkle.

One elderly lady saw me and grabbed me. "Now, you mustn't get ill. 'Cause you're ours, you see." Her words were suddenly picked up by the crowd. "Yes, you're ours."

The emotion clutched me by the throat and two sloppy tears welled up behind my eyelids. I was proud to belong. It was that same feeling the crowd in Cornwall had expressed. Someone believed in me. I felt I had an awful lot to live up to.

It is a truth that most people want to see you smiling, whatever sort of hell is going on inside. If you're cheerful, it cheers others. If you try to come up smiling even though they know you've been through some dreadful storm. I try to remember that always. How right those words are that they sing on the Kop at Liverpool. I suppose almost everyone has forgotten that they come, years ago, from a musical called *Carousel*, so closely have they been adopted by the Liverpool fans.

> When you walk through a storm,
> Keep your head up high.
> And don't be afraid of the dark.

I try to remember that always.

Chapter Four

My great mate Peter Dudley helped me through some of my blackest times. I first met him twenty-six years ago, at a time when I was absolutely down. He became what I used to call my little clown. He was always laughing or coming up with some gag. He is a terrific actor too, and I think it was the ambition of his life to be in *Coronation Street*. As a member of the cast he was well-loved.

But Peter has had more than enough trouble of his own and then illness struck him suddenly and savagely. Granada were as helpful, kind and understanding as they could possibly be, and Peter struggled on manfully but he was slow to improve. Finally, it was decided that it was best he should leave the Street for a while until he could perhaps fully recover. I wish him luck and feel always for him as a friend. Knowing Peter, I'm sure he'll succeed in beating the illness.

I have specially warm memories of the hilarious times he and I and the rest of the gang shared on holiday – our annual trip down to Cornwall. The advertisement had said: "Large, quaint farmhouse in secluded area, hidden by trees. Sleeps twelve." It slept six at most. There was an old dairy the owners had termed the playroom. It was that exciting, we christened it the mortuary. The whole place had an air of neglect.

It was a black, blustery day when we arrived and everything looked so dreary. As usual, organising Annie started moving everyone around, trying to cheer the place up. "Those tables there," I said to Ernst, pointing to some rickety pieces of furniture dotted around the room. "We'll put them together and cover them with a sheet if there's no tablecloth."

I spotted an old five-bar gate outside, hanging off its hinges. "Right. Outside," I said to Peter. "We'll get that chopped up for a start. They'll never miss it. A roaring fire in the hearth will do wonders for this place." The gang and I set to. A couple of hours later the house looked a little more inviting but Peter was convinced it was haunted. If it wasn't then, he made damn sure it became so.

I remember one evening we were all sitting there after dinner. Talking and dreaming. Dusk was drawing in and we had switched on the lamps. Suddenly, the place was plunged into total darkness. There was a weird choking noise coming from the mortuary. We sat there, paralysed with fear. Then there was a giggle that gave the whole thing away. Peter had tiptoed quietly out to the mortuary where the power switch was and turned off the electricity. Then he'd started moaning and gibbering – Peter playing ghost.

Every night there was some different excitement. Tapping on windows. Torches glimmering in the undergrowth. One night Nell and I went up to our room to find Peter had made us an apple-pie bed.

"Never mind," I told Nell. "Just ignore it." We got into bed. We'd been talking for several minutes when suddenly I said: "Shhh. What's that strange noise?"

"Aaaah. Aaaah."

It came from somewhere down below us. I looked at Nell, signalled her to stay quiet and hung over the side of the bed. And there, there was Mr Dudley, in a large picture hat and with an artificial lily in his hands, lying stretched out under our bed. He'd been there for almost twenty minutes.

He frightened himself so much playing ghost that he actually started to believe the house was haunted. One night when the rest of us went out and left him alone, because he didn't feel like going, we returned to find him white-faced and shivering. With his vivid imagination he'd scared himself to death.

Life with Peter was a series of very funny happenings. He made me laugh when there was no laughter about with his crazy antics. He also understood me very well. I can be very restless on holiday. Always wanting to be off, to explore new places. One morning I announced to the crowd: "Let's go to Pixie Cove today." We packed picnic hampers and set off. But when we arrived, I wasn't so sure.

"Mmmm," I muttered, looking around deep in thought.

"Don't anybody unpack anything," Peter told the others. "We'll be here exactly five minutes. I can tell by the look on Her face."

Sure enough, a few minutes later. "I don't quite like this cove today," I said. "Let's move somewhere else."

We piled back into the car and drove further along the coast. Stopping at another beach, we played the whole scene again. Still, I felt, the place wasn't quite right. When we'd stopped at about three different places, with Peter warning everyone every time: "Don't get anything out of the car. She might change Her mind," I finally settled on a beach. Why, I don't know. There was a force eight gale blowing and we sat wrapped in towels waiting for the sun which She assured everyone would be out in a minute.

"It's got to," Peter said. "It daren't disobey Her."

Whatever happens in the future between Peter Dudley and me, I will always carry close to my heart the laughter and loyalty that he gave me. In any case, we will always be friends. Always friends. I know Peter Dudley as a very warm human being who made me laugh when I really felt like crying. Who set out to be my own personal court jester, to bring the smiles back to my face.

I think we've only ever had one row and that was when he was driving me to some public appearance. We got lost on Spaghetti Junction – Birmingham. My sense of direction is terrible. Peter says he is spiritually guided to the right place. However, we still got lost. Every time we stopped the car to ask the way, someone would say, "Oh, it's 'er. And she's with 'im."

Consequently, we couldn't get any information from anybody. It got later and later. People were so busy asking for autographs they took no notice of our pleas for directions. We finished up screaming at one another at the tops of our voices. What the row was about I really don't know. But, we missed the appearance. By the time we found our way it was too late.

We were later to do that date again. It was a terrible time. There was a knife fight outside the hall. Peter said to me: "I knew we were fated not to come here in the first place."

Ernst Walder is another old friend who helped me a great deal after Alan's death. I first met him on the Street when he was brought in to play Elsie's son-in-law, Ivan Cheveski. We became good friends and kept in touch after he left. He settled in Yorkshire, dealing in antiques and still playing Nazi generals and officers – which was rather ironic considering how oppressed his native Austria was during the war.

Ernst is Mr Rock-solid. He never changes, remaining always loyal to his friends. It's amazing, after twenty-five years in this country, that he still has his Austrian accent. I'm constantly correcting him. But it was useful on occasions. So often I've seen him smile at policemen and say: "So very sorry. I am a stranger een your country," if he's been caught parking in the wrong place or some other minor traffic infringement. And our lovely British bobbies usually wave him on understandingly.

We used to tease him unmercifully about his accent. But Ernst was totally good humoured about it. In fact, recently he was telling us how in one television programme he managed to play the whole of the German army. He had one role but ended up doing the voices for all the soldiers. In effect, he was the German army.

Some time after Alan's death, when I had picked myself up and begun to dust myself down, I agreed to do a play. I became interested again. The excitement, the planning of starting a new play is wonderful for taking your mind off everything else. Ernst was to come with me, touring Canada with *My Cousin Rachel*.

I remember one very hungry-looking Canadian lady who set eyes on the four beautiful men of our company. Unable to resist them, she invited us back to her private pool and sauna bath. We accepted and it was a very nice afternoon. We had a marvellous time. But I couldn't help but notice her eyes looking longingly at the fellas. Finally, steam rising, from the over-heated pool, she approached me. "Er, which one is yours, honey?" she asked.

I saw the light of lust in her eye. I turned my head and winked at the boys, then back to her. "All of them," I said with great solemnity.

There was a moment's pause. "Aren't you the lucky woman," she said, bitterly.

After she left we fell on each other, laughing. The boys confessed they were absolutely terrified of her. She was one of those overwhelming ladies who kept insisting and insisting and insisting. There was one worrying occasion when she asked Ernst to fix a lightbulb in her bedroom. He came tearing out, begging for protection.

I did a lot of the protection act in Canada. Perhaps it was the climate at that time of the year and in that part of the country. I think it was something like twenty degrees below zero while we were in Yellowstone. That's where we were touring around Halifax and Nova Scotia. Every time a lady said: "Isn't he just divine," we closed ranks. I'm sure everyone must have thought I was a very active lady, very energetic. I felt rather like Mae West in her old age, trailing four beautiful fellas who danced attendance on her.

Ernst has recently returned to Austria. He plans to set up a holiday farm there and has bought a place about one hour's drive away from Vienna. It's in a beautiful valley, wonderful for skiing in the winter and long, leisurely walks in the summer. When his holiday farm is ready, you can be sure I'll be a frequent visitor there.

Peter Adamson was a source of great comfort during the time of Alan's troubles. Peter, too, had been through alcoholism. He had gone to the edge of the abyss but, unlike Alan, had fought his way back.

I love Peter like a brother. We worked very closely together in the early days of *Coronation Street* at the time when he was on the mend. He had bad times then. But once he'd come out of the wilderness he never stopped trying to do good for others.

He visited Alan in hospital on several occasions and tried to help. But Alan would never accept that he had a drink problem. Peter was to tell me later that he saw Alan shortly before he died.

"He was in a shocking state," he said. "It was as if he'd been beaten up." I learned later that is how alcoholic poisoning affects the body.

I had no real experience of alcoholism then. Peter, of course, had had first-hand experience and tried to help by passing his knowledge on to me. Every time I became despairing, wondering what I had done wrong – questioning myself, "Is it me who's driving Alan to drink? Is it my fault?" – Peter was there offering comfort and wise words.

"It's no one's fault," he would say. "Alcoholics are born

An historic shot taken on the first days of rehearsals for a new programme –
Coronation Street. Things have changed a lot since then.

The moment the viewers saw on screen as Alan and Elsie said, "I do."

Our wedding day. Alan and I expected just a few close friends, instead there was a crowd of fans outside the church. (© Roy Broome.)

With Alan on a television show in 1975. We were still touring then in Britain. Eleven months later I was back in the *Street*.

Me and Alan in costume for *Gaslight* at the end of our British tour with the play in 1973. Shortly after, we left for New Zealand.

Sunday Mirror

16p   September 9, 1979   No. 853

THE TRUTH ABOUT ME and ALAN by Elsie Tanner

PLOT TO KILL THE POPE

The Pope—threatened

A SECURITY source has revealed to the Sunday Mirror a plot to kill the Pope.

It was the same source which warned in March that Tory MP Airey Neave was doomed to die

The Tory Ulster spokesman was blasted to death in his car at the House of Commons just three hours after Scotland Yard were told by the Sunday Mirror of the IRA plot against him.

This time it is Protestant fanatics who have drawn up assassination plans.

They aim to kill Pope John Paul when he visits Ireland at the end of the month.

Disappeared

An intelligence chief said in Ulster: "We know the Loyalist paramilitaries are planning something big. We have good reports that the Pope is the No. 1 target."

Five known Protestant hit-men have disappeared from their usual Belfast haunts in the past few days.

Security chiefs fear that these men are on their way to the Irish Republic via the English mainland to avoid the current massive security clamp-down on the Irish Border.

Two Protestant squads are

Sunday Mirror Exclusive

believed to have marked the Pope down for death.

One of them has been recruited from the illegal Ulster Freedom Fighters who have promised to make the IRA pay in blood for the murder of Lord Mountbatten on Bloody Monday two weeks ago.

The other is believed to consist of a group from the official Ulster Defence Association who are equally enraged at the slaughter of Lord Mountbatten and eighteen soldiers.

Worried police chiefs in Dublin have drawn up the tightest security precautions ever for the three-day visit of Pope John Paul, which starts on September 29.

They have also asked the Royal Ulster Constabulary to trace any known Loyalist gunman who has disappeared from his usual haunts.

A police spokesman said in Dublin yesterday: " Our force

Turn to Page 5

CORONATION Street star Pat Phoenix told last night why she did not go to the bedside of her dying husband, actor Alan Browning.

Pat, pictured near her holiday home in Cornwall with Peter Dudley—who plays Bert Tilsley in the Street — and former Crossroads actor Ernest Walder, left, said: "People must have thought I didn't care.

" But it's not true. I am desperately, desperately sorry he is dead."

Alan and Pat had lived apart for two years.

My Grief—Page Two

Win a Mini! — Page 7

GEORGE BEST COMING HOME — Page four

With Peter Dudley and Ernst Walder on the front page of the *Sunday Mirror*, taken the day I heard of Alan's death.

With Ernst Walder on our British tour of *My Cousin Rachel* in 1979.

A *Street* party to celebrate our two thousandth episode, which was screened on June 2, 1980. That's me waving behind Helen Worth who plays Gail Tilsley.

Michael Foot, Tony and me at the unemployment march in Liverpool in November 1980. It was so cold that day I wore my fake fur coat. The newspapers later described it as "opulent fur". I ask you! (© *Liverpool Daily Post and Echo*.)

Tony's an avid Liverpool Football Club supporter and he couldn't resist this opportunity to kiss the League Championship trophy after the club won in the 81-82 season. (© Harry Ormesher, Southport.)

Summer seasons are lovely, and our show in Eastbourne in 1982 was no exception. We took time to do all the touristy things – walking on the prom, seeing the sights and soaking up the sun.

A surprise party for Tony's birthday last year (1982), and all our friends joined in the celebrations. I bought him an exercise bicycle which Chris Quentin, Tom Pendry, MP for Stalybridge and Hyde, Tony, Ernst Walder and Peter Dudley made me try for size.

thirsty, m'dear. But be careful. Be very careful. 'Cause in the end, you know, alcoholics not only take themselves down, they're inclined to take all that they love down with them too."

Peter has had more than his share of trouble – it seems to pile on top of him. But whatever hand life deals him, I have known the gentle, kindly side of Peter.

In some ways, particularly in personality, he and I are two diametrically opposed people. He is not an extrovert like me. As an extrovert I am aware sometimes I can be irritating. Let's face it. Though many people may like, even love Pat Phoenix, there are those who can't stand the very sight of her. Basically, I think, because at one time I was perhaps too energetic, too full of minor explosions. People have been known to say: "Go away, Phoenix. You wear me out." I think there have been times when I irritated Peter in that way. I can be very wearing, particularly if I'm full of health and ready to go, go, go. I've been told that I have great turbulence. I disturb the air about me. The people who love me like to think it's angel wings. The people who hate me think it's a devil from hell itself.

I seem sometimes in my intention of honesty, to put my foot right in it. There was that time Lynne Perrie invited me to her new flat for a drink. Now, Lynne is not a bit like Ivy Tilsley, the part she plays so well. She is quite glamorous, the world's loveliest giggler and a wonderful hostess. When she gives you a drink, she pours you half the bottle.

I was talking. I didn't notice she was filling my glass again and again with champagne. I must have had about three big glasses full. Looking round the room, which had become slightly swimming, my eyes rested on a particular painting.

"That's a bloody awful picture, Lynne," I said.

She was shocked. I don't normally swear and I must have seemed so rude. "Why?" she said. "What do you mean? It's eighteenth century . . . docks somewhere."

"I don't care if it's the bloody tin mines. It's a terrible picture."

"Oh, I'm sorry you don't like it," she said defensively and obviously rather hurt.

The friend I was with spoke up quite loudly. "I think we'd better go, Pat."

"Oh. Do you really think so," I said.

We left. In the early hours of the morning, after the effects of the champagne had worn off, I realised how much I had insulted her about her choice of pictures. The painting had obviously been upsetting my subconscious and I had blurted out what I'd been thinking. The next day I went out and bought her an oleographed copy of an Old Master and delivered it to her at Granada. Which prompted Geoff Hughes to remark: "Pat, you can insult me any time."

After that the running gag for days was: "Go on, Pat. Please insult me."

"No, no. It's my turn. Me."

Lynne is madly impulsive. One Sunday morning I got a phone call. "I'm on my way, dear." It was Lynne. "I'm coming past your house. I've been baking for you. There's one pizza, one chocolate cake, one fruit cake and two dozen fairy cakes." What chance have I got of keeping my weight down with friends like that?

She arrived on the doorstep bearing the goodies. Her hair was still in rollers and there was a smudge of flour on her nose. "You'll have to take me as I am. I've just finished baking." That's Lynne, a lovely person.

I've a terrible habit of walking into my friends' places and moving things around. They don't call me Organising Annie for nothing. I walked into Lynne's flat one day, noticed another picture which I thought looked out of place and said: "Oh, no. You can't have that there."

"Whose flat is this, anyway?" she said. She even got Johnny

Briggs in on the act. Johnny's part-time working abode is the flat upstairs. Lynne called him down. "Johnny, Pat says that picture can't stay there. It's wrong."

He ended up knocking in nails all around the place to move all the pictures, grumbling: "Whose flaming flat is this? Yours or Pat Phoenix?"

I'm a typical Sagittarian – speaking my own mind, not always tactfully, and assuming people will appreciate that it's for their own good. It isn't always well received.

Lynne Palmer, who played Martha Longhurst in the Street, was a very attractive lady and adored hats. She had lots of them, usually very pretty. One day she made the terrible mistake of buying one of those horrible leather, upturned po contraptions. Very fashionable at the time. She flounced into the Green Room at Granada, did a couple of twirls and said: "Do you like it? Don't you think it's nice?" Everyone said politely: "Yes, lovely."

She looked at me and said: "You haven't said anything. What do you think?"

There was a pause. "I think it looks bloody awful."

"What! I've just paid the earth for this hat," she said.

"You've got a million and one pretty hats," I told her. "Did you really have to pay out good money for that upturned chamber pot you're wearing? It does nothing for you and the hat's an abomination."

She sulked for ten minutes. But afterwards she kissed me and I never saw the hat again.

Chapter Five

The crowd on the Street are a hard-working, valiant, loyal, talented cast. However much they are praised, they could never be praised enough for their total dedication to the show. They are seldom, if ever, able to escape from public life. They have on many occasions been the target for knocking campaigns in the lesser newspapers. When there is no news *Coronation Street* is always a good bet for a front page story. The whole of human life is there.

We are, in fact, sitting ducks. If one of us should behave like a human being, say for instance get a parking ticket or spill his soup in public, that could make at least three columns in the Daily Howsyerfather. We are not difficult to find. Nor is the Street where we live. God knows, we're not saints. But I have to say we're not heavily into sin either, at least most of them aren't. And anyway, what is it people say? "To err is human. To forgive is divine." My God, have I made some "er . . . er . . . ers" in my life, and I ain't alone.

It could happen on any occasion. It could be sitting down, when the opinion of many is that you should be standing up. That's wrong for starters. It could be writing a jokey letter to girl students, and having it taken seriously. That's wrong. It could be a couple of actresses even going so far as having a slanging match in public. That's very wrong.

There is nothing new in any of this. Since the start of the

theatrical profession, actresses have been known to have cat fights in dressing rooms. Letters have been written – some of them *belles-lettres*. Articles have appeared in the newspapers. But when it's all boiled down, what is it really? A lot of theatrical gossip.

There is a story that goes back in time of the rivalry between two famous actresses, one of whom was Sarah Bernhardt. Her rival, in an attempt to hurt her, stuck pins in her toilet soap. That sort of thing doesn't happen today. They do it with words.

But when some slightly knocking article appears in the press something strange happens among the ranks in *Coronation Street*. We close up and shoulder arms. In other words, become highly protective of one another. I'm not saying we're all bosom pals – only some of us. But we do try to stand by each other.

There are many tales told of actresses who demonstrate verbally and in no uncertain manner their anti-feelings for Phoenix. There is one lovely story, often told at dinner tables. I wasn't present, so I don't know for sure, but the story goes that this certain lady turned purple with rage at the announcement of a forthcoming play I was to do. "How dare she! How dare she!" the lady said.

A friend of mine who was in the company was heard to say: "That lady has forgotten more about acting than you'll ever know."

The argument became more heated. "I know for a fact," said the lady in question, "that Pat Phoenix was a convicted prostitute in Barnsley."

As the story goes, my friend slapped her, however slightly. She left, with much huff.

I knew nothing about this particular escapade and was to know nothing about it until two years later. The story came back to me by way of several old friends. I never knew the details but I learned that the argument was over me. I wasn't particularly curious. I had been out of the country at the time and it is not unusual for people to say things about others in our profession. But two years later, a well-meaning young friend of mine heard the story first-hand from my friend. She came to me with a look of absolute horror. She repeated the story, finally getting to the punchline. "And do you know what she said? She said . . . " my young friend gasped. She couldn't bring herself to say the words. "She said you were a convicted prostitute in Barnsley."

I am very fond of this young lady and I don't quite know what reaction she expected from me. Probably not the one she got. I fell off the chair laughing.

"Well. Prostitute I don't mind. But Barnsley . . . " I said. "Barnsley? She could have upped me a bit. Not that I've anything against Barnsley, but, well. . . I mean, it doesn't add to one's reputation of being a prostitute, does it? Particularly a convicted one." I didn't stop laughing for three weeks. I never repeated the story to the lady in question. Why should I? It was my particular secret, and it just illustrates the point – you don't have to be loved by everybody.

But I've had plenty of good times on the Street. Strange thing about *Coronation Street* – some people stay for years, some people leave and come back again. It's a place to return to. It's a sort of home. I've had many friends who've passed through the Street. Somehow, sometime, I know they'll either be back or we'll meet again somewhere. Diana Davies is one of the dear friends that one day I hope I'll work with again. Cheryl Murray too. I had great fun with her and Veronica Doran – Elsie's lodgers – and we worked closely together. Cheryl is madly generous and impulsive. She's a Leo of course. She understands me a lot better than most.

We did have one terrific row. I can't even remember the details now but I do know it was a storm in a teacup. One of those occasions when we were both fed wrong information by other people. I ended up storming at her: "With friends like you, who needs enemies?" But it was all sorted out in the end and we're the closest of friends these days. She left the Street once before, several years ago, to have a baby. She has the most beautiful baby daughter. I was glad to see her return. But as Susie Birchall is what is known as a floating character in the Street, her contract came to an end and she had to leave again. I expect to see her back pretty soon.

Veronica Doran, who plays Marion Willis, is leaving too. She is very sweet. A true blue. We all three had great fun together. On the Street the girls were supposed to argue terribly. Off screen they were almost like sisters. On set doing a row scene, there was all that hatred being emanated. But when it was over they'd throw their arms around one another. And we shared a long-running joke. I was Mama, they said. They'd burst into song: "When Mama gets married, we'll live in a house. Oh, Mama, get married today." It was a send-up. They did all the bits from *Gypsy*.

I'll miss their fun. Like the times they'd crowd into my postage-stamp-sized dressing room for a quick cigarette between scenes. Three of us – four if I had a visitor – all puffing away in that tiny room with no windows. The air was blue – with smoke, not curses.

Cheryl joined the gang on a holiday in Cornwall one year and I don't think she'd ever laughed so much in her life. One day we were all out in the car. There were so many of us, we were crammed in like sardines. We pulled up at a bus stop so some of us could go shopping. After a while we were all back in the car except Cheryl.

Peter Dudley was with us. He can go into an act at a moment's notice. He saw Cheryl walking towards the car, got out and grabbed her by the hand. "Wait till I get you 'ome. You little bitch. You've been at it again, 'aven't you."

Cheryl looked around wildly, hoping no one would recognise her. There was a queue of people waiting for the bus watching all this. I've got my head down in my coat collar, hiding my face and the rest of them in the car were hysterical.

"Your mother and I 'ave been sitting 'ere for half an hour," Peter shouted at her. "Get in that car."

"What. I was—" Cheryl tried desperately to get a word in.

"Don't you speak to your father like that. Get in the car." Peter slapped her legs and shoved her, head first into the car. He carried on shouting at her in the car.

By this time the people at the bus stop were staring open-mouthed. "Eh, isn't that Bert Tilsley. And isn't that Elsie Tanner, hiding in the back?"

When Peter goes into one of his acts he does the voices, the faces, the actions . . . the lot. He looked like a little old man, shouting at Cheryl. We drove off, all of us laughing hysterically, leaving behind an astounded bus queue wondering what the hell had hit them.

The cast of *Coronation Street* are a great crowd. I like 'em all, almost without exception. It's like a roll of honour. There's Johnny Briggs, who plays Mike Baldwin – a smashing bloke, one you can rely on. Then there's Bryan Mosley – Alf Roberts – another whom I respect a lot. He has tremendous optimism and has been a great comfort to me at times. And there's Chris Quentin – Brian Tilsley – a vigorous and lively young man now most intent on studying his profession.

There was the great Liverpudlian wit of Geoff Hughes, who played Eddie Yeats; Fred Feast (Fred Gee) who loves the horses – and so do I; lovely Jack Howarth, MBE as he is now, who plays Albert Tatlock. He does marvellous work for charity, day after day; Bernard 'Bunnie' Youens (Stan Ogden) who was in his heyday better looking than Clark Gable and had almost as many women swooning at his feet; Teddy Turner (Chalkie Whitely), a thoughtful, gentle, super man, kind to everyone; Bill Roache (Ken Barlow), the philosopher in the Street.

Thelma Barlow, who plays Mavis Riley, is perhaps the lady I envy most. She's artistic and domestic. She makes jams, tends herbs. She sews beautifully and is a superb cook. Jean Alexander (Hilda Ogden), too, has incredibly green fingers. Everything she touches grows.

There's Anne Kirkbride – our Deirdre Barlow – a very pretty young woman with a great sense of humour; Betty Driver (Betty Turpin in the Street), a very warm person, a great animal lover; Eileen Derbyshire (Emily Bishop), a lovely, delightful lady and very, very kind. There's the wit of Julie Goodyear (Bet Lynch) and the comedy of Jill Summers (Phyllis Pearce). I first saw Jill doing a charity variety act at a Lady Rattlings ball. She was the funniest woman I've ever seen on stage. Doris Speed (Annie Walker of course) is the bridge champion of the Street and dedicated to the game. There are the factory girls whose warmth and friendship I adore – Helene Palmer (Ida Clough), Elizabeth Dawn (Vera Duckworth) and of course lovely Lynne Perrie (Ivy Tilsley). Liz Dawn is an extremely beautiful lady but hides all that beauty under her grimaces and comic faces.

There's little Helen Worth (Gail Tilsley now), a smashing actress. We had great fun, Cheryl, Helen and I when they all lived at Elsie's house. I'm almost sorry she married and moved – in the storyline that is.

Esther Rose and Julian Roache – two of our writers – I have the greatest admiration for. Eric Rosser, our archivist, has all the history of *Coronation Street* at his fingertips. Bill Podmore I have known for years and years. I've seen him come up from being a cameraman on the Street – a very good cameraman – to his role as director and now executive producer. I always feel, rightly or wrongly, slightly maternal towards him. He's a great guy. Seems strange to think that now he's become one of the father figures of *Coronation Street*.

As I said, I like them all, almost without exception. Everyone works damn hard for every sort of charity. When the newspapers are writing knocking stories about us they usually omit to say what an enormous amount of good the cast do for charity. They are, on the whole, caring people who are entitled to some little respect. Everyone's keen to knock. I don't think it's ever been worked out or written down how many millions the cast of *Coronation Street* have made for charity.

In the wake of the newspaper stories comes what we all call the idiot fringe mail. Letters, not many I'm glad to say, that are usually full of obscenity and abuse, and we have a special way of dealing with them. Whoever they're about, we read them out loud and then pin them on the notice board at Granada for several days while everyone has a good laugh. And some of them *are* funny. I'm still getting letters asking for pictures of me in black suspenders or bathing costume. I ask you!

The situation wasn't improved by our move to temporary rehearsal rooms which looked directly on to the Street itself. It was almost like being in the monkey house. The odd members of the public who strayed onto the Street by accident would catch sight of us and say: "Oh, look. They're in there." Whereupon one of us would call out: "Kindly do not feed the animals through the bars."

The rooms were in a listed building with workhouse windows that wouldn't open and very little natural light filtered through. After the big, airy rooms we used before, it was like putting the birds from my aviary into a tiny cage. Nothing like the marvellous rooms we had left. They assured us it was only temporary. In the move the famous plant given to the cast of *Coronation Street* by Noel Dyson (who played Ida Barlow) went with us. It didn't like the new rehearsal rooms either and began to fade and wilt. Only the kind attention of Jean Alex-

ander and Betty Driver helped it survive through that period.
The plant has been with us for so long now, it's become a part
of our folklore. Superstition has it that if the plant dies, so will
Coronation Street. Well, it is still with us but its growth was a
little stunted while we were in those rooms.

There's a lovely story which, I think, sums up the character
of the people in *Coronation Street*. Betty Driver, Fred Feast and
Julie Goodyear were filming a comedy sequence where they
were all out for a drive when the car ran into a lake. They were
assured they'd have a car lined with a fibre-glass tank so they
wouldn't get wet. When they arrived for the filming all they
actually got was plastic bags – dustbin liners. It was a bitterly
cold day and they were in the water for three hours. They were
all absolutely frozen.

To add insult to injury, when they finally got out of the car,
Julie was supposed to fall into a cow pat. Not content with
having her fall into any old cow pat, the director was there,
very busily pouring water on to one particular cow pat to
make it soggy enough and messy enough for Julie to fall into.
When she stood up after her fall, she had liquid manure on
more than her skirt. It was running down her legs, her hands,
everywhere. The day after they were all absolutely shattered.
Yet Betty and Julie were both saying how super it was, in all
the adversity of the day, to be together and have a joke.

That says something about the Street that they managed to
laugh their way through it.

I have great friends, too, behind the scenes on *Coronation Street*.
The directors, the writers, cameramen, soundmen and technicians. There's Vinnie, my favourite props man of all time. We
share a long-running gag. He was a great *Soap* fan and so
suddenly within the confines of the Street set, and in sharp
contrast to the north country accents, there'd be a Southern

belle drawl. "Why Benson. Would you mind gettin' me a mint julep."

Roughly translated, that's me asking Vin to fill up my glass with what looks like gin and tonic – only looks, I never touch the stuff – for a scene.

"Why Jessica. Ah sure will," he'd say.

There are my two regular make-up girls, Julie and Sarah, whom I miss very much if they are away at any time. They bully me no end.

"Oh, my God. Look at this. Had a heavy night last night, did you?" they say. "Never mind. I suppose we can do something with it. Just keep yer head still, that's all."

They also ask me the most direct questions sometimes. One day recently Julie bent down and whispered conspiratorially in my ear: "Hey, listen. Y'know when you got chased around and fellas used to try and get you on the casting couch. What did you do? I mean, you can't be rude, can you, if it's somebody important or powerful?"

"Oh, there's one infallible way of stopping them," I said.

She leaned even closer, eager for advice. "What's that?"

"We used to say to them, 'I think you're adorable. Delightful. But I've got this terrible rash that keeps coming out on my top lip. I'd love to . . . But perhaps we ought to wait until it clears up.' The men used to back off in terror," I said. "It never failed."

We both fell about laughing. In truth the casting couch was a problem for actresses – and actors – even in those early days. We had to handle the situation with kid gloves.

I have this habit when they're doing my hair of fiddling with it. It annoys Sarah terribly. As my hand reaches up to tweak a lock of hair she'll draw herself up to her full height – she's not very tall for all that – and say: "Righty-ho. Righty-ho."

I can see the tension mounting. "All right. Don't get uppity," I tell her teasingly.

There are so many people. The girls on the switchboard whom I adore, secretaries, people throughout the building for whom I have great affection. After twenty years of knowing them so closely, who could help it. If I omit to mention some in this book, it isn't that they're forgotten. There simply isn't room.

People like the lovely ladies of the wardrobe without whom we couldn't function. One of them, Noreen, bosses me about a certain piece of jewellery I wear – a multi-cut diamond on a gold chain given to me as a present. I wear it all the time and forget I've got it on. On set, running through a scene, Noreen shouts, "Your damn diamond's slipped again," and rushes on to sling it round the back of my neck again where it can't be seen.

"It's a fake," I tell her. She doesn't believe it one bit.

Noreen was off work some time back and that diamond was seen on *Coronation Street* twice.

Things often look better on screen than they really are. I have a constant battle with the directors over Elsie's clothes. "You look too glamorous," they once said. Too glamorous? I was usually wearing some tatty thing bought specially for the Street or some of my own very old, very worn-out clothes.

"If Elsie's supposed to have been in the rag trade nearly all her life," I argued, "she'd never go downhill as far as clothes are concerned. She's always been a bit over the top." There is always one in every street who's dressed up to the nines. I heard a remark once that sums up Elsie perfectly. "Look at 'er. Bloody rabbit fur up to the armpits and no knickers."

But the writers wouldn't agree. They decided that all Elsie's clothes would be ripped up by a jealous female whose husband she'd been going out with. That left Elsie with two blouses and two skirts. But they hadn't reckoned on her having to go to a few weddings and other big dos. Gradually the clothes have been replaced.

Viewers, too, are quick to point out things they think are wrong. We had a letter once complaining about the real crocodile handbag someone was using. It was plastic, the worst sort of plastic croc you could find.

We were all in our character costumes on the day in 1982 when the Queen came down our Street. She was there to officially open the new set and we were all lined up outside our respective houses waiting to be introduced. The official party, the mayor, Chief Constable Anderton, our chairman Sir Denis Forman, the Queen and Prince Philip, made its way along the line and stopped at me.

I can never reveal exactly what was said between Her Majesty and me. Suffice it to say it wasn't just what I told the press later. After she and the rest of the party finally moved away, the reporters closed in. "What did she say? They were with you longer than the others. What was it all about?" they asked.

"We talked about the dogs," I replied. The rest is my secret.

Chapter Six

Clothes were an important asset to an actress in the early days of repertory. I was never out of work at that time because I had a fabulous wardrobe. I could find the right clothes for any part. Most of them were second-hand, mind you. Because I learned to buy from second-hand shops, I have a passion for them even now.

When I was with a company in Bradford we found a marvellous second-hand clothes shop called Smith's. 'As bought from the gentry' the sign over the door said. For a pound you could get a complete wardrobe for a play. Pure silk dresses and furs included – all a bit moth-eaten but they looked superb from the auditorium. Harry Hanson, who we worked for then, was a great stickler for wardrobe and we used to spend our time in that shop. We were on good money – well, £19 a week was good money then. Out of that you had to buy all the clothes needed for each part. If it called for riding breeches or negligees of the posh silk kind, you had to have them and we found them in Smith's. We also learned to make our own props. I can't sew but I could put together anything. Even now, I can tack together a ballgown that would last the week and then fall to pieces. In those days we could make a hat appear in the same play in fifty different guises. False eyelashes were very expensive and only really seen in Hollywood, but we could make them. We pulled hairs from our heads, each one knotted separately to make false eyelashes as good as the film stars'. We also used something called hot black – a type of mascara that we heated and blobbed along our eyes. We had great blobs of mascara which from the front looked fantastic.

A leading lady was sometimes employed according to the length of her hair. Managements preferred it at least shoulder-length so that it could be dressed in ringlets or in a full period style if the play demanded. All of which we had to know how to do ourselves. I used painter's gold dust in my hair to turn it blonde, Armenian Bole to turn it brighter red, flour to go grey. I've greased it, soaked it and sugared it. Sugar and water makes a sort of hair lacquer – stiff as a board though. It's a wonder I've got any hair left at all.

The old reps were a finishing school in a way. Not quite Roedean – but they did teach you practically everything about life in high society. How to set banqueting tables correctly, how to keep silver – and polish it – how a maid should carry a tray. We had to do flower arrangements, tart up our own clothes, wash and iron them, and usually the fellas' too. We learned to cook a little, how to make do and mend. A little French, a little Latin, a few good manners.

I have a great interest in clothes. I did a little designing some time back and I'd like to do more one day. I can't bear to wear the same thing two days running. A friend said to me during the Alan period: "You're ill. You've worn the same dress for two days." She was right. I had. That went against all I had learned in rep. I had a good teacher. A man called Arthur Reece who was a strict disciplinarian and a wonderful producer, later to move on to Bristol Old Vic. He had red hair and a temperament to match.

One morning at rehearsal his temper snapped. "You are supposed to be something different. You are supposed to set standards," he addressed the cast. "When the public come in here at night they see you beautifully dressed and made-up.

They believe you are really like that. Ladies," his voice reached full pitch, "I do not wish to see slacks on my stage or any of you coming to rehearsal in curlers or unmade-up. An actress should look as good at 10.30 in the morning as she does at 10.30 at night."

Harsh words but what good training. Even now, if I feel deathly in the morning, I still make my face up. When I went to work at Granada someone said I looked as if I was dressed for a personal appearance every day. Well, yes, I have to do a personal appearance every day. Every time the public see me out in the street, getting out of the car or shopping, they don't expect to see me looking like a drab. I may feel like it sometimes, but I'm not about to let everybody know!

The days in rep were hard and frugal. But we were young and found something to laugh about in the most difficult situations. Even when we were traipsing the streets, cold, wet and hungry – we were always hungry I remember in those days – looking for digs, we could joke about the 'glamorous' life of the theatre.

Oh, what digs! I remember now with horror some of the terrible places we stayed in. On tour we usually arrived at night in the town we were playing next. The women teetering along on high heels, wrapped in thin macs and lugging enormous suitcases, we'd set about finding somewhere to stay. I always knocked on the doors of houses where the windows gleamed and, inside, people sat round a roaring fire. I could never knock at houses where the curtains were drawn tight.

Not that my choices were any better than the others'. "Let's try this one," I'd say, calling to another member of the company who was probably about to knock at another house opposite. I'd knock on the clean but shabby door and some weird woman would fling open the door. "Eee, well just call me mam," she'd say. More unlike your mum you'd never see. She would probably have a few curlers in, looking rather like Hilda Ogden. Inside, the house would be like the Ogdens' too.

We often stayed in what in those days were called 'combined chats'. A room with a gas fire, a bed, a rickety table, a chair and one armchair. Lights were out at twelve o'clock so we always kept candle stubs so we could learn our parts late at night. We wouldn't get home from the theatre until almost midnight and the room would be cold. If I had enough coppers for the gas I could manage a couple of hours by the fire, straining to read my lines by flickering candlelight. We had to study into the early hours of the morning, doing one play a week. Playing one and learning another at the same time.

The lavatory was always down the garden, what seemed miles away. If I shared with a mate in the company, I used to say she had a weak bladder. I'd wait until my friend was halfway up the stairs, then turn to the landlady and say: "I'm sorry to bother you, Mrs Bloggs, but my friend has a terrible weak bladder. I wonder, could she have a po?" Treachery indeed! But the idea of traipsing down four flights of stairs and outside into the garden on bitterly cold nights was horrifying.

On the rare occasions when the house we were staying in actually had an inside loo, the situation wasn't any easier. I remember Anthony Booth and I, an old friend called Bill Ridout and the stage manager, all being in terrible digs where the loo was right upstairs – through an old lodger's bedroom. We were all up late one night, reading through lines with a couple of bottles of beer to keep us going. At four o'clock in the morning we all wanted to go to the loo. We made a plan. The four of us would go up together and the last one out would pull the chain. There we were, like four Pink Panthers waiting in a queue to go to the lavatory. Each one in turn tip-tipping across the room while the lodger snored on in bed. The last one went in. A few minutes later we heard the chain being pulled and saw him dash out and run like hell down the stairs while the old man sat up in bed spluttering.

Sometimes the landlady provided supper – usually something indigestible like beans on toast or cheese on toast. Other times the digs were self-catering. On one occasion we were supposed to be cooking for ourselves. The cupboard was bare, we were broke and we weren't due to be paid until the end of the week, so we raided the landlady's pantry. But it had been well cleared of everything, probably to stop us pinching bits. All that was there was a packet of spaghetti, Colman's mustard, Ovaltine, flour, HP sauce and a tin of Cherry Blossom boot polish. I took the lot and mixed a sauce. It looked terrible when I'd finished so I added a touch of boot polish and the sauce came up a nice black-brown colour. We poured it over the spaghetti and ate our meal, if not with relish then, at least, with gratitude.

Some places only did breakfast, which we always missed because we'd been up so late the night before studying. That meant there wasn't another meal for your money that day. Thank God for the soup kitchen where we could get a good bowl of soup for a few pennies.

At the end of one season my weight was down to seven stone two, so you can imagine we weren't very well fed. I think that's where I learned to smoke heavily. Cigarettes filled you up. And they were cheaper than food then – certainly not the case today.

We were always glad when someone asked us out to supper after the show, which they did very often, thank goodness. It kept us floating. The rest of the time we lived in the theatre. Rehearsals in the morning, back to the digs for a nap if possible, returning to the theatre for the evening performance, then back home, to start studying all over again. That was our life.

I didn't do the things other young people did. How could I? I was always working. I never went to dances or played tennis.

I still can't dance to this day. My life was totally taken up with the theatre. It was what I always wanted to do. As a young girl I had a burning ambition to work in the theatre but no money and no apparent means of getting out of the trap – the very poor, lower-working class – that I was in. There was no escape route, no drama school for me. I was one-track minded, determined to act, and I was able, finally, to go the way I wanted. But it took me a long time.

Once there I wasn't about to lose any chances by going off on any jaunts or by being ill. You weren't allowed to be ill or have a breakdown. In this business you have walking breakdowns when people say: "What the bloody hell's the matter with her?" I remember I worked with a leading man who had tuberculosis. He was terrified the management would find out. I worked with him for years and he had the most terrible coughing fits. If the management had known he had TB, he would never have been employed, in case he ever had an attack and be unable to appear.

I've played on stage with gastroenteritis, with blood running down my hands, ripped by flying glass from a bottle broken on stage. But the show always went on. In some ways I don't think I could ever go back to those days. I can do a tour with one play but I doubt if I could ever learn a play a week again as I did then, one grande dame after another.

I was a fey thing then, totally wound up in the characters I played. In Keighley on the Yorkshire moors, I played the part of Catherine Earnshaw in *Wuthering Heights*. I wasn't just playing Catherine, I was her. Every minute of spare time I spent up on the moors. Listening to the wind wuther and finding my way across to the ruin that is Wuthering Heights. I'd fly the moors – hair down my back, long skirts and totally unsuitable sandals on my feet. I became lost in my dreams.

That was how I missed the chance of meeting Orson Welles. A company was doing some filming up on the moor and for some reason Orson Welles, who was with them, stopped at the old Silent Inn on the road to Stanbury. He was still there when I floated in off the moor. I ran across the room, long hair flowing, eyes dreamy. I saw the large, portly gentleman standing there and just passed on in my misty way. He turned to the old lady who ran the place and said: "I believe I've just seen Catherine Earnshaw herself."

The locals told me later that some big film star had been up there filming. "A fella called Welles. Some'at Welles." I missed him. I was that dazed and fey I didn't recognise Orson Welles when I saw him.

There is a lovely story told in Hawarth about the Black Bull Inn. In the main room of the inn, there's a chair, which, so the story goes, was Branwell Bronte's favourite. He always sat in it and it was always pointed out with some pride to new visitors. But even though Branwell's chair had been sold to visiting Americans many times . . . there always seemed to be another in its place.

Chapter Seven

The course of acting, particularly in the theatre, doesn't always run true. So often something happens that shouldn't. Half the fun, and the skill of working in the theatre is to overcome these minor disasters – sometimes even major ones – without disturbing the tenor of the play too much.

Gaslight, in which I toured with Alan, seemed plagued with problems. It's one of those big dramas, a thriller in which the tension mounts higher and higher as the action unfolds. By rights, the audience should be on the edge of their seats, all eyes on the actors throughout. We played almost every possible date in this country and then took it to New Zealand for three and a half months. Nearly everywhere something went wrong.

There were hilarious nights. Nights when the gas went up when it should have gone down, or down when it should have gone up. Nights when vital props were forgotten or when they broke on stage.

Norman Wooland played Inspector Rough for the British tour and he was a dream to play opposite. We had great fun together. On one occasion we were playing a theatre somewhere in England and had reached the part in the play where Rough tells Mrs Manningham the truth about her husband. There we were on stage, face to face, and Norman was supposed to say: "Mrs Manningham, your husband is a homicidal maniac who thinks you are getting to know too much."

What he actually said was: "Mrs Manningham, your husband is a homosexual maniac who thinks you are getting too much." I stood there for a few seconds aghast, with Norman wondering why I was spluttering and choking with laughter.

Another time we were appearing in Kirkcaldy. There was a bomb scare and they had to clear the theatre. The place was so small, the cast ended up standing outside on the pavement in full costume talking to theatregoers. We must have looked strange. Bella Manningham chatting amiably about Scotland to the visitors. The evil Manningham strolling peaceably up and down the pavement. Eventually we were allowed back into the theatre and started up the play again.

On stage, Norman looked at me and said: "We've done this bit already." We started again and reached the part – a very tense moment in the play – where Rough has to say: "What time does your husband return, Mrs Manningham?"

At that very moment the theatre cat, a great fat tabby, decided he wanted to cross the stage. Over the footlights. The cat was so big, he found great difficulty in stepping over the lights. Norman and I stood there transfixed. The audience's attention was rivetted on the cat too.

"Urrumph, rrumph." The cat struggled over the last footlight and went off stage. The whole trip must have taken him at least three minutes. Norman repeated the question: "What time does your husband return, Mrs Manningham?"

"Oh, just in time to put out the cat," I replied. That finished everybody. Well, what could I do? I couldn't ignore it.

One of the most important props in one particular scene of *Gaslight* is a brandy flask. On one night of madness Norman came on stage without it. Halfway through his speech he muttered to me in an aside: "I've forgotten the bloody brandy."

Ad-libbing, I rang the bell for the maid. And again, and

again. Eventually I shouted for her, "Elizabeth, Elizabeth."

She came on stage looking rather flustered. All this wasn't in her script.

"Inspector Rough is feeling the cold. Will you bring his scarf from the hall," I proclaimed. Then out of the corner of my mouth, " . . . and the brandy flask from his pocket." We finally got the flask to him. I don't think the audience noticed the ad-libbing. At least, I hope not.

Props are a constant worry to an actor. Will it work? Will it fail at just the wrong moment? When things go wrong, it can be in the most spectacular manner.

Scenery and backdrops are usually stored on stage, hauled up into the flies out of sight of the audience. The theatre in which we were playing had just finished its Christmas season and the pantomime flats had been run up into the flies above us. I was on stage, just about to go into Mrs Manningham's big, dramatic speech at the end of the play. Manningham is trussed to the chair and Bella says: "You monster. What you did to me . . . "

At that moment there was a rustle like you've never heard before. Fifteen tons of tinsel and glitter fell in shreds from the ceiling and covered Alan who was playing Manningham. I had to part the stuff covering him head to toe before I could deliver my speech.

You can never be certain of anything on stage. If the part calls for a character to say something won't happen, you can bet your life it will.

Alan was tied to the chair and Rough had to say: "There, I think that is secure. You may talk to him now, Mrs Manningham."

At that point the chair collapsed in bits.

This year Tennessee Williams died and I mourned deeply the loss of a brilliant writer. I must have appeared in nearly all of his plays – and there have been so many wonderful parts.

To my mind he was one of the greatest writers ever. He was a man who understood the intricacies of a woman's mind. Most of his ladies suffer in some way, and I don't identify with that, but I believe those roles are the nearest anyone has ever come to really understanding the feminine mind. It is never as it seems. No woman has just one face. She has many faces – a touch of this, a touch of that and a touch of something else. Like filigree. He created roles with which the average woman can identify, no matter that they are set in the Deep South. His characters are not one-dimensional. They reveal layer after layer after layer, in every speech.

He wasn't well regarded everywhere. In my naivety I once put my foot right in it – and lost the chance to play at the Abbey Theatre in Dublin. My agent asked me to go over to the city to play in the farce *Tons of Money* opposite Frankie Howerd. It was all very sudden. The leading lady had become very ill and I was asked to step into the role at the last minute. I flew over in the morning and gagged my way through it on stage that night. After the performance I was asked to join the management and the local priest for a drink.

"You were wonderful, Miss Phoenix," said the priest. "Would you come back in another play? Any play. Whatever you choose," he said magnanimously.

Innocently I said: "Tennessee Williams' *Rose Tattoo*."

Teddy Palmer, a friend from way back who was also in the company, gave me an almighty kick on the shin.

The priest coughed, embarrassed, and shifted slightly in his chair. "I'm sorry, Miss Phoenix. That play is not done here."

"Why ever not?" I asked. Teddy was still kicking me under the table.

"Because there is a certain article dropped on stage," he said, referring to the contraceptive packet which is dropped on stage at one point in the play. It is not seen and certainly never named. But purely because it's there the play was not allowed in Dublin. I thought that was terrible. *The Rose Tattoo* is a beautiful play, a real love story. There is nothing offensive in it.

I never did play at the Abbey and don't suppose I ever will.

However much I enjoy working with *Coronation Street*, the battle is always on between television and the theatre. I suppose my first love has to be the theatre. How could it not? All my early life from the age of eleven was spent in the theatre. It's in my blood. I love the very smell of it, the draughts in the dressing rooms, rehearsal rooms so hot you're sweating. It's show business to me whereas television has always seemed much more of a business business.

It's part of my life to make contact, to communicate. All part of acting. I'm just a strolling player, out to tell the people stories, to enchant them, to make them happy or sad. In the theatre if I can feel peoples' emotion I can hear them draw breath. I can't hear them on television. On stage you can be Anastasia one day and Lisa Doolittle the next. Your range of accents must be enormous and you must know your craft. In television that is not essential.

I suppose because my basic training was in theatre I always think of myself as a stage actress. Even now, some of the things I do in the studio are totally theatrical. I forget about things like overhead microphones and cameras and the like. If a script calls for a chair to be crashed down, I'll crash it. I think it's more real that way. Then I'll remember the overhead boom. "Oh, no. I'll have to do that again." If I have to rush through a room, on stage I'd move as fast as possible. In the studio the movement has to be slowed down to one-third of that pace because the cameras can't keep up.

When you see Elsie telling off one of her girls on the screen, they appear to be facing each other. But in reality I'm yelling at a camera while she's well away in another part of the room yelling back at yet another camera.

"Now look. If you do that again I'll smack your face for you. I'm telling you once and for all," Elsie can yell on screen. It looks very dramatic. But the girl she's yelling at isn't really there. I find that totally devastating.

On an opening night in the theatre, the place is alive, buzzing. Behind the curtain I can feel the audience's high, almost read their thoughts. I can tell if I'm going to have to get out there and make them listen. I can tell if they're going to be enthralled and attentive. It all depends on the actors – not on cameras. It's absolute line-to-line contact. In television it's never that.

So my mind is in conflict. I love the theatre. I love television. When I'm in the theatre for a long run I want to be back on *Coronation Street*. When I am in the Street for a long time I want to return to the theatre. Either way I don't think I could manage without doing some theatre fairly regularly.

I adore the whole business of acting. The creating of something vast. I can't sit back in the dressing room waiting for everything to be made ready. If something needs doing, I'll do it. If there's a nail sticking out of a chair, I'm just as likely to grab a hammer and pull it out. The unions these days don't like it very much – there's the right man for every job – but my training in rep means I can't help it. It's an automatic reaction.

I remember on tour when the wrong props arrived at the theatre for the play we were doing. Instead of having a dress rehearsal I put my hand in my pocket and sent the entire cast propping with the cash round every Victorian junk shop they could find. I bought yards of green baize and bobbling. We spent hours sewing those bobbles on, I remember, to make the curtains. What mattered to me was that the set looked right. Nothing else.

I remember the play, *The Miracle Worker*, for a different

reason. It had such hope, a tremendous message at the end. It was the most moving play I've done in years and I think it was for the audience too. Wherever we played there was an enormous audience of deaf, dumb and even blind people who came with their 'ears' or 'eyes'. I learned to sign the deaf language and used it for my curtain speech as well. People came round in droves to see me in the dressing room after the show, delighted someone had bothered to learn their language. I felt very humble.

The conflict goes on. I love the theatre and I love the Street. Perhaps my ideal would be to have three months away from *Coronation Street* every year to do something in the theatre that could be prestigious for the Street and for me. The world knows that actors thrive on change. It's refreshing and they return ready to attack their major roles. They see things from a new angle. They are alive and sparkling.

And I think it has to be said that, however much the world owns Elsie Tanner, the passions, the integrity, the pride, the arrogance and the weaknesses all belong to Pat Phoenix.

Chapter Eight

Coronation Street has been called many things by many people. A soap opera or a folk opera. A great panacea or the national dummy as I often think of it. Some people love it, a few hate it. But always it has a very special, loyal following from people living in Coronation Street homes themselves, right through to university students and professional people. The Street is, I believe, essential in some ways to our British way of life. You may find it funny to say that about a mere television programme, but it has done more for the people of this country and others than viewers or critics ever realise.

They should see our mail. We are Marjorie Proops, Claire Rayner, all the agony aunts rolled into one – at least those of us who bother about the people who write to us. There are thousands who live *Coronation Street* because they've nowhere they'd rather be. Life has been perhaps too harsh for them or they are alone. But then those old friends keep popping out of the box. So there is no way I could ever knock *Coronation Street*. People do – the actors in it do. We're its severest critics but it is criticism meant to improve, never harm.

In the early days Philip Lowrie, (who played Elsie Tanner's son Dennis), Ernst Walder (who played her son-in-law) and I were a closely knit family. At rehearsal I used to say: "We've got to work for each other. We've got to watch each other, criticise and help. That way we'll be the best." And we were.

When we all started on *Coronation Street* most of us were television raw and theatre fresh. When we went on the screen we weren't experts in television technique, any of us. We only knew one way to act. And act we did. I think we broke the glass. *Coronation Street* went into viewers' living rooms with all the guts, the fervour and the love we had for the programme. In those days it was a one-off. Original and as near as you could get to the truth about that section of northern people. So much so that, for a long while, people thought of some of us as the characters we played in the series and we had to work very hard to get them to think of us as actors again. Still people ask: "Are they really like that?" I have to say they are extremely good actors doing a damn good job of work with love and affection.

Coronation Street has a community that lives, works, eats and sleeps together, and remains as a community. We have the threat of nuclear war over our heads, the land is being torn apart, polluted and destroyed, and yet the people of *Coronation Street* continue to go their particular ways. I think it is this very community spirit which holds people to the programme. In these uncertain and unsettling days, it is something constant in their lives. Other series, the American programmes in particular, are about the rich and privileged. *Coronation Street* shows poor people, working people, and how they go through life. Things are often black and there may not be much money but somehow they find their share of happiness. They have their tragedies, but they have their comedies too.

We all of us owe Tony Warren, the creator of the Street, a great deal. He is a genius, a man ahead of his time in everything he does. Some of the things he writes can be slightly shocking because they are truths that are obvious for everyone to see and yet are seldom spoken about. He is someone of whom I've always been very, very fond and nothing can ever break that friendship. We may not see each other for months, even a year, but we maintain that close understanding. He writes me marvellously witty letters and always signs them "Angels guard you." I hope they guard him. Tony Warren disappeared for a time after he left the Street. I think people deserted him rather. I didn't. He used to call me his first star. He said so in his book, *I Was Ena Sharples' Father.* "Noel Coward always had Gertie," he said. "I've got you, Pat."

I have grown old on *Coronation Street.* There have been two decades of children growing up since it first began. People come up to me and say: "Oh, I've been in love with you since I was two years old." They've grown up now and I've changed too. I used to speak reasonable English at one time but I've spoken North Country for such a long time now that it stays with me. My accent shifts. It can be "frightfully naice" one minute and the next slide into "cum 'ere you".

The blame for my back trouble can, I'm sure, be placed squarely on Mrs Tanner's rounded shoulders. Years ago Anne Cunningham, who played Elsie's daughter Linda, and I talked about building character. How we would walk and stand. "They'd lean," said Anne. "Lean at every conceivable moment. After all, they're both basically sluts." That meant arms folded and shoulders hunched. I've been doing that now for twenty-odd years and my back has suffered accordingly. The only time I really straighten up is when I'm at home or out at a function somewhere.

In some circles *Coronation Street* has become something of a cult. It's easy to see why. After twenty-two years the programme has become almost Dickensian in content. It has become a classic. Certainly not a soap opera, very possibly a folk opera. Whether I stay with *Coronation Street* for the rest of my life or – could be the fates decree – I leave tomorrow, it has taken much and given much. It has filled my life for twenty-two years.

After twenty years *Coronation Street* was looking a bit battered. The set has to stand up to a lot of wear and tear. When parts of the Rovers started to come away in our hands, Granada decided it was time to build a new Street.

Without all the publicity that went with the opening of the new set, viewers would never have realised anything was different. The new Street looks on screen an exact copy of the old one. The props department work hard to keep it that way. They are always running round spraying and dusting down the set to make things look older and tattier. Most days at least one of us is in trouble for looking too posh. It's difficult. However tatty things look in real life, on screen they always look glossier and better.

I was accused recently of coming on set with a hairstyle like the wife of a British ambassador. All I'd done was ask the girls in make-up to put it back like it used to be, in a curly chignon. Mrs Tanner wore it like that for some time in the early days but styles have changed. Today it looks too dressed, too elaborate for the Street. When I walked on set there was consternation.

"What the hell d'you think you're doing?" All around me faces were staring in amazement and some in horror.

"Pardon?" I asked in all innocence.

"Your hair. It must have cost all of £40 to do."

"But I've just had it done upstairs. It's—"

"Put it back the way it was."

That was that. There is no way Elsie could go back to her old self, often much to viewers' disappointment. She could wear her low neck, satin frilly blouses and short, tight skirts with slits up the back then. It was all the fashion. Today if I were to put that same Elsie on the Street everyone would say she was over the top.

There are certain differences on the new set – but only those working there can spot them. The old Street wasn't wide enough to get crane cameras, cables and all the modern equipment down comfortably. The houses were just exteriors with a very rickety bannister round the back if we had to be seen leaning out of upstairs windows. The new set is built round a big shed into which all the doors of the houses lead. If at any time they want to build a set or part of a set inside, they can do so.

The road is much wider and lighter. The cameramen and technicians can get better tracking, better shots all round. We used to call it the Street where the sun never shone. It was long and narrow. Even in the hottest of weather there was always one side in darkness where the sun couldn't reach. The situation is much better these days. The Rovers actually looks like a pub to people visiting the new set. They can see inside to the bar. Scenes in the Rovers are still done in the studio though, so there is no change in that respect.

Viewers could never tell which shots were done on the old set and which on the new. The improvements are in the technical side of things. And the Street will last much longer. The show is seen all round the world these days – even in Haiti – and it's also out on cable television.

There's another benefit in the new set – for the actors at least. Now there's somewhere to run for cover when it rains. The cameramen insist that rain doesn't show on film unless it's pouring down. They're right, it doesn't. All the viewer sees is the wet street. That doesn't stop us getting wet. It's nice on the rare occasions to be able to open a door and step inside.

Filming outdoors can be heavy-going – constant interruptions, stopping for this, that and the other. But there's always the lighter side. For instance, when the soundman has to fix a microphone, and it always has to be hidden somewhere under our clothes. "I'm very sorry, luv. I'll have to go up your blouse again," he'll say with a grin. In the middle of the street – all very public – there's this rather nice man with his head stuck in my bosom and his arms around me. It looks anything but what it actually is.

Rarely can we get through a take outdoors without some interruption. A member of the public gets through the net, unaware that we're filming. "Eee, Elsie. I've been watching you for years. Now . . . " Or a woman opens her door. " 'Ave you done. Would you like a cup o'tea?" Bang. We have to go back to the beginning again.

There was one day I remember, very windy and cloudy. It was one of those days. They were trying to match shots with those already taken – a quiet, sunny Sunday on the Street. First of all the sun went behind a cloud. We had to wait for it to come out again. We started filming again and an airplane came into the shot. Then a lorry and then, finally, someone started sandblasting on a nearby building. Everything went wrong that day. We had to find time somehow that week to cram in the lost filming.

We're used to distinguished visitors on the set of *Coronation Street* but one of the nicest of all was Dustin Hoffman. He was absolutely charming and worked terribly hard. There was a very funny moment when he asked me if I was the sex symbol of the show.

"Well, I used to be," I said. "But I'm not quite sure now what I am. I think I'm probably more the tired old tart these days."

Part Two

Chapter Nine

"The actor Anthony Booth, well-known for his film and television roles, in particular the series *Till Death Us Do Part*, is seriously ill in hospital today with third degree burns after an horrific accident at his home . . . " The newscaster carried on impassively with the rest of the day's news but those words raced around my head. Tony? My old mate from repertory days with whom I had shared so many hilarious times and even a hectic but passionate romance. I couldn't imagine him lying there, fighting for his life.

Over in the hospital Tony was hearing the same broadcast. He had been admitted only hours before and was lying in great pain, literally burning up, and flitting in and out of consciousness.

"Wake up, wake up, Mr Booth," the nurse said. "You're on telly."

He turned his head to see his picture on the screen of the ITN News. He passed out again, only to be woken up by the same nurse.

"Quick, quick. You're on the BBC too."

"And then I knew I was in trouble," Tony told me later. "If it was on the BBC as well I must be dying."

Tony's wildness in those early days in the theatre I found very attractive. He had a great infectious laughter about him and used to do utterly mad things on impulse. I remember in one company we had a great character actress called Velvy Attwood who was seventy or more then. Tony used to fling open the door of her dressing room and say: "I want you, Velvy, more than anything in the world. Come to me, my darling."

There was Velvy in her long combinations and her vest saying: "You are awful. Get him out. He's horrible."

He did it for devilment and Velvy, frankly, enjoyed the attention.

We first met way back in the mid-fifties when I joined the company in a play called *A Girl Called Sadie* which was later to become famous in its way for earning managements more money than had ever been done before. I was the leading lady, earning all of £19 10s a week and touring all over Britain. Tony was playing the vicar with the task of trying to reform me, the fallen woman. That was on-stage. Off-stage he was hotly pursuing me.

The cast met for the first time in a cold, bare rehearsal room. I saw this bold, quick-witted, energetic boy standing with a group of other actors. In my time I may have been called a controversial, outrageous lady. Then I was more than a little old-fashioned in my outlook on life. Boys had to be well-behaved and show proper respect for girls. Tony had no awe and no respect, or so it seemed at the time.

I was blonde then. The management had insisted I go silver-blonde for the part of Sadie and so my red hair had to be dyed – much to my mother's consternation. That was all right when it was first done but after nine months in the play, constantly bleaching my hair, it started to fall out. My hair was down to my elbows when the tour started. When it finished I was practically bald. I had a Yul Brynner bubble-cut. By that time Tony and I were romantically involved. He used to say he was going out with the only bald leading lady in the business.

But that was later. At first I backed off from his advances.

Just out of my first disastrous marriage, I felt I wasn't going to be caught again. Tony, nevertheless, set out to woo me heavily – when he wasn't playing practical jokes on me and the rest of the cast.

We had a marvellous old man with us, Louis Nanton, who played the doctor. He had to open his doctor's bag on stage every night and say: "I'll get the stethoscope out and see to the patient." One night before he went out, Tony filled the bag with all sorts of rubbish – empty cardboard packets and papers. The old man nearly had a fit when he opened it.

But most importantly, Tony made me laugh at myself. He made me realise how ridiculous I could be and eventually I did succumb, to his sense of humour and his passion. But not until – with the perverse streak that is in my character – he had given up. The moment he stopped chasing me, I changed my mind.

That was the start of our love affair. Our wild and frantic romance. We were both young, without a home or very much money, but we were madly in love. Too much so, perhaps. We were both too fiery, too unbearably on the go at that time. We would have burned one another out had we stayed together.

Tony left the company to go into *No Time For Sergeants* while I remained touring with Sadie. He would finish work on Saturday night and somehow get from London to wherever I was playing. On one occasion he was found climbing in through a bedroom window at the place where I was staying. On another he flew back from Rome to see me.

Time went on and we began to go our different ways. I joined another company, still touring, while Tony was hitting the big time. For three years we drifted further and further apart. Three months went by without a word from him. Proud as ever, I tossed my head and went off. But still I couldn't lose sight of him. He was doing well in films – and earning himself a reputation as a tearaway. I was constantly reading in the newspapers about his antics. I knew Tony and understood all this. Others didn't. He is a lot like me. The thing that leads him into trouble is his directness, his honesty. I recognised a kindred soul. Like me, he tried to fight the establishment for very good causes and for others rather than himself. Like me, he usually finished in some sort of trouble.

I read stories of his wildness. Stories that he drank a lot. As it turned out, he didn't drink a lot, but he got drunk very quickly. He had a sugar deficiency – three pints and he'd be absolutely drunk out of his head. When I saw the stories I said to myself: "That's ridiculous. Tony doesn't drink." He didn't. None of us did in those days. On a Friday night the company might have a bottle of beer apiece to celebrate the end of the week, but that's all. I couldn't even touch the stuff now.

I could not connect the Tony of these stories with the man I knew. A man with so much life in him. Lively people like him don't need drink. They've got their own source of energy and excitement. Nor could I connect a dying Tony with the man I had shared a grand passion with all those years before. In any case love was the last thing on my mind as I thought about Tony. I was still wounded mentally, and I knew Tony was physically – though not to what extent. He was just a friend in trouble and I wanted to see him.

But would he want to see me?

Since we'd parted, we'd seen each other only once, many years later, on the set of *Coronation Street* when he came in to play Christine Hargreaves' boyfriend. He was tied up emotionally with someone else and so was I. We barely spoke. When we came together again, later, Tony told me he thought I was snooty. I thought he was distant. We were both retaining a distance through pride.

I knew he'd been living with someone for many years and there were children. Perhaps I would be intruding if I visited him? Twice I came very close. The first time, on my way to a public appearance with my friend Keith, we drove near the hospital where Tony was. Time was short and we couldn't stop. The second time I was with a girlfriend. Should we stop and see Tony Booth, I asked?

"If he's the guy you say he is, and if he's burned about the face, he may not want to see you," she said.

We drove on. I wish now we hadn't. To see him was not meant in any romantic way. I just felt perhaps he might need a friend. As it turned out I didn't know how much Tony needed a friend. In all the time he spent in hospital, apart from his children, his sister and Una Stubbs, no one visited him. No one. He was very much deserted by others he'd thought close. If I'd obeyed my instincts and gone to see him I think it might have helped. I don't know. Certainly he did have a very bad time.

Several months later I got a phone call at the studios. It was Tony.

"Hello Pat. It's Tony, Tony Booth."

"Oh, how are you?" I said, delighted to hear his voice.

"I'm fine, fine. I'd like to see you," he said.

"Well, why don't we meet for lunch next week. At the Film Exchange here in Manchester."

I didn't know. I had no idea of his circumstances. First of all, he had no money at all. Secondly, he could hardly walk. A wind would blow him over – he was down to seven stone. But when I saw him at the Film Exchange he was well dressed, he was groomed. Absolutely super. I noticed he wore fingerless gloves on his burned hands.

"Hello Tony," I called across the room. "Lovely to see you. How are you?"

"Oh, all under control," he said, dismissing his horrific injuries with a wry grin. "But what about you. How are you?"

I'm a great believer in fate – that enormous plan that controls all our lives. Part of that plan for me was that Tony and I should come together once more. Why else should I think of him so many years later? Why else, when Tony desperately needed someone to talk to, someone who would understand, should he be reminded of me? But in the beginning it was just friendship. We talked a great deal and I began to understand a little of what he had gone through.

"What you really need is some publicity," I told him. "So that people will know Tony Booth is back, fighting and ready to work. Come and stay at my cottage overnight. We'll call in the press to do an interview. You know – an old mates' reunion."

"Yes, fine," he agreed.

He came, fell in love with the cottage and we talked half the night away that first evening. He was living at his mother's house in Liverpool but conditions weren't exactly ideal.

"Why don't you come and stay here until you finish the book you're working on. There's plenty of room. We won't get in each other's way," I said.

He agreed to stay but only as a working and paying guest. Of course, in some ways I was wary about his coming to stay. I wanted no romantic entanglement and told him so straight. "We're just friends, right Tony? No hanky panky." I didn't really think he'd be interested anyway. We'd put too much distance between us.

There were always friends coming and going. I was living my life, dashing off all over the place. I thought there would be no problems like that. Tony needed someone to talk to. He was starved of theatrical conversation. He hadn't worked as an actor for about two years before the accident. So he missed actors' tales. I'd come home at night, usually shattered by the day's rehearsing or filming, and we'd talk and talk. Curled up in a chair in front of the flickering fire, I'd tell him of my day, things that had happened at the studio.

One evening, on Kitty my housekeeper's night off, I was greeted by delicious smells coming from the kitchen. I walked through and found Tony, wooden spoon in hand, preparing dinner.

"I'm chef tonight," he said. "And I'm a good one. It's time you allowed someone to spoil you – you don't eat enough."

The meal he served was superb. There was wine for me and orange juice for Tony. He swears he will never drink again. He doesn't even like the taste any more. We talked of old times, laughing over old memories. Both of us had a different view of each other. He told me how haughty I'd been in those days. He reminded me of things I'd forgotten about myself. Things I deserved to be reminded of. He talked about what had happened to him, his experiences in hospital. Even then his burns were unhealed and yet he turned his tragedy into laughter. I was filled not with pity but with sympathy and admiration for his courage.

I think it was laughter very close to tears – but he laughed all the same rather than cry. I found myself warming to him. We had the same views on so many things. Our faith, our love for the theatre and for the job I was doing and he could not. Tony felt then that he would never work again. He told me frankly about his live-in girlfriend by whom he had two children. Why he had stayed when he hadn't wanted to. And how, in the end when he desperately needed support, she left him. And he told me about the accident. It is an horrific story, one that sounds almost unbelievable. But it is true because I know Tony to be totally truthful. He had no reason to lie about it.

He was introduced one night in a pub to two men who said they were SAS. Tony was interested because he was gathering material for a book he was writing. They talked and drank and eventually returned to his flat. Tony told me he wasn't drunk. It was only 10.30 in the evening. The door of his flat was locked and Tony couldn't get in. But the SAS men had an idea.

"Y'know what we do when we want to get 'em out? What we do, we get a bit of old rag and paper, stuff them all round the door and set 'em alight. The smoke goes in and they come out like rats. It causes no damage," they said.

"Don't be ridiculous," said Tony. "There're kids in there." Not expecting for a moment that the SAS men would carry out this absurd threat, Tony looked around for another way into the flat. There was a way in through the loft so Tony climbed up. Halfway along his foot slipped and went through the ceiling. He saw great clouds of smoke billowing up from below. The SAS men had carried out their plan.

Tony called to his children: "Quick. Open the door. Get out, get out."

As he jumped down from the loft he saw great sheets of flame and fell into a five gallon drum of paraffin stored on the landing for their heaters. He went up like a torch, burned to the waist.

At that point one of the men ran away. The other stood there as Tony rolled down the stairs – a human torch. A neighbour heard Tony screaming and came to help. The SAS man told him, "You'd better send for the ambulance." Just then Tony collapsed.

In the hospital his clothes were cut away. But while his boots remained on, his feet were literally boiling in paraffin. When they were eventually taken off, two of his toes had gone.

While in intensive care he had about thirty skin grafts to rebuild his legs and feet. The extent of the burns was massive. Tony tried to prevent me seeing the scarring in the first weeks at the cottage. But he couldn't hide for ever and one day he told me he had to have a bath.

"So?" I queried. It never occurred to me that he couldn't get in the bath by himself.

"Could I ask Kitty to help me?" he said.

"Don't be so silly. I've been married twice. I've seen it all before."

"You've not seen this before," he said, referring to his burns. I wasn't worried about seeing them. Scars and burns didn't make any difference to the person, the person who lived inside.

He wore a strong elasticated one-piece garment which held the flesh together and was designed to stop the worst of the scarring. That had to come off first and he had to be helped into the bath. I'm no nurse at the best of times and I like my baths hot. Unthinkingly I drew the water and, wearing a sort of kimono dressing gown against any splashes, prepared to help him in.

Tony was still very underweight but he is over six feet tall and I'm not all that strong. I know I look a large lady but in my stocking feet I ain't so big. I took his arm and tried to let him down into the bath slowly. I nearly went into the tub with him. I had to let him go with a bump, straight down into steaming hot water. Tony screamed in agony. He looked up, once he had recovered himself. "Phoenix, I'll never recommend you as a geisha girl."

Chapter Ten

Somehow along the way I've gained the reputation of a firebrand. Someone who's always ready to lash out verbally against injustice. I hate to cause pain and I hate to see it inflicted by anyone else. In situations like that I always feel I have to intervene – which doesn't lead to a quiet life.

For many years at Granada it was always me who stormed up the stairs if something was amiss, demanding it be put right. Harry Kershaw used to say, "Someone makes the bullets and you fire 'em. It disturbs the tenor of your life."

That's my particular madness. Having said it, I'd go forward even for the sake of rotten bravado. There are times to be silent, of course there are. But me being Irish, I don't always observe those times. Someone once told me: "It's time you got off your white charger, Pat. It's always you who runs into the windmill." They were right but I think I'm still in the saddle at times.

When two inspectors came into my house to investigate my right to a widow's pension after Alan's death, I charged full tilt. Tony doesn't live with me. His home is at his mother's house. He does stay at my cottage a great deal – it's in a better situation to look for work and there's plenty of room. I often have friends staying for months on end. But somehow they had it down in their little black book that he was living with me. In their eyes, therefore, I wasn't entitled to that pension.

They marched in one clear, bright morning, a man and a woman, to investigate.

"Are you cohabiting with Mr Booth?" they asked.

"What do you mean?" I asked in my most imperious manner. I wanted them to actually say what they were thinking.

It turned out that, putting it bluntly, I could have it off on the village green opposite the house, but not under my own roof. I pointed out that I had spare rooms in my house and I had a couple of actors and actresses staying at the time.

"Am I cohabiting with them as well?" I asked. "People come to stay here for a week, six months, longer sometimes. If they're out of work or in some trouble, I've always got room for them. You should be giving me an extra allowance for keeping out-of-work friends."

"You see," said the woman, rather embarrassed, "we don't think that women who aren't married should get away with the privileges that married women have — "

"What privileges?" My mouth dropped open.

"Well, does Mr Booth do little jobs for you like carrying buckets of coal or driving your car?"

"Most of my men friends have driven my car for me from time to time. I ask it as a courtesy and I hope they continue to do so. As for carrying a bucket of coal, I hope any man here would offer to do it. I'm very old-fashioned like that."

"Well, we believe it is unfair that — "

"Just a minute." I was beginning to burn with anger. "I supported my last late husband for nearly three years. Really, you owe me that money, don't you?"

The money doesn't matter a damn to me – they take it away in tax in the end anyway. But all the time I was putting myself in someone else's place. Perhaps someone who wasn't working, who relied entirely on that pension. God damn it, in my heart of hearts I am that woman. Yes, I'm working. But any day, any day in my life I could become that woman. Tomorrow I may have no job. Tomorrow maybe I will need that pension.

It's all so unfair. Do you know that a man, if he's a widower and lives on his own, can have as many women as he likes coming in and out of his home without the pension people bothering him? That's allowable. He's a man. But a woman can't. Imagine, a woman on her own finds a boyfriend, or just a friend, after her husband has died, and he comes to stay, perhaps only for a visit. They can stop her widow's pension. Ain't that great?

The female inspector was insistent. "Would you say you were living together?"

"Well, if that's the case, I'm also living with four other people," I said. "And as for Tony and I sleeping together, certainly not. We're Catholics and we're engaged." What else could I say, what could I do? Only fight fire with fire.

Talk about sex discrimination. They were only doing their jobs, those people, and were very sweet in the end. But that situation of widows and widowers must be changed. Such discrimination in this day and age!

I'm a very open person. Some would say a blabber mouth. I don't see the point of telling lies. Evasions, yes, when you want to avoid hurting someone but never downright lies. My mother forcibly evicted lies from my life. I got walloped every time I told stories. I was a great imaginer, a romancer going off in flights of fancy. I'd come home and tell the story of what had happened in the street. Two people would develop into two hundred, their actions growing with the telling of the tale. I think because my father had been an expert liar and a charmer to boot, my mother was dead against it. If ever she felt I had gone over the top, I got a belt.

She had a quote she always rattled out at such times, something about: "You can watch a thief, but you can never watch a liar." Sounds Irish to me! She was later to regret her strictness when I became so truthful it was an embarrassment at times. Details of things at home she'd rather have kept quiet, if someone asked me I trotted them out innocently. It is something that has stayed with me throughout my life. Of course, like everyone else, I deceive myself but that's not counted. Lies in human relationships do, and they are a complete waste of time.

I'm a great truster. Sadly I'm learning not to be quite so much these days. I am a simple person and my life works simply. When I ask why can't the starving millions have the butter mountain and the surplus corn, it's no good people saying to me: "That's economics." What the hell do I know about economics. All I know is that when something is obviously wrong, someone has to try and put it right.

I always feel, wrongly of course, that everybody thinks as I do. Management surely will not be upset if I tell them the truth. They are bloody upset, nine times out of ten. Like all typical Sagittarians, I tell the whole shell of the story and forget about the kernel. I go to speak to someone in authority assuming they are on my wavelength. That they are going to understand, even before I finish my sentence, what I am talking about. And, in reality, do they? Hardly ever. They look at me with blank faces as I blow up for the sake of some principle. How bloody expensive those principles are. I've lost opportunities, jobs, money because of them.

Elsie Tanner occasionally comes out with some wise words in her down-to-earth, no-nonsense way. I had a lovely line to say recently. It was at a council meeting where everyone was arguing over whether to allow a disco or not. Talking about some of the councillors, Elsie had to turn and say: "Don't they make you sick. They get weals on their bottoms from sitting on the fence."

There are times in this life, I believe, when you have to stand up and be counted. The unemployment march in Liverpool three years ago was one of those occasions. Tony and I took part not because we wanted to be seen by the press and the public but because it was something we both believed in. We wanted to register whose side we were on. We ended up standing with Michael Foot on the lorry heading the march – by coincidence, not out of publicity-seeking in any way.

We didn't tell anyone we were going, just arrived in the city that grey, blustery, bitterly cold morning and joined with the marchers. We were simply two faces in a crowd of thousands. It was so cold I wore what I call my beauty-without-cruelty coat – a fake fur – for warmth. The next day it was reported in the papers that Pat Phoenix had worn an "opulent fur coat" for the jobless march. It was fabric, for heaven's sake. And it had a rip in the back as I remember.

Under a cold, heavy sky with black clouds gathering, the march set off. Tony was still very, very tottery on his feet and walking badly but nevertheless determined to do the whole march. The atmosphere was tremendous. People of our own profession were there, Equity and the musicians' union, as well as people from other professions walking side by side with unemployed people from all over the country.

Michael Foot had broken his foot and so was riding on the back of a lorry with other Labour ministers. They spotted Tony struggling in the crowd.

"Tony, hey Tony. What are you two doing down there? Come up here," they called. We climbed aboard the lorry.

That day in Liverpool amongst all those people was one of the most moving experiences of my life. The square by Liverpool's Pier Head was packed with a sea of faces. I've been a socialist all my life but people were accusing me of being a fair-weather socialist. My heart then, as today, was with those marchers. I wanted to be there.

People say: "Oh, don't get involved. Do keep quiet. It'll

only cause you trouble." Yes, it will cause me trouble. But it will cause me terrible trouble with my soul if I don't speak out.

You know, people are very careless of their souls. To me a soul is a small beautiful child in a locked room somewhere in your head. Very often people forget to feed it. It needs feeding very much. In this day and age souls get trampled to death very quickly because of the "don't get involved, don't speak up" brigade. "You might get in trouble," they say. You might do this, you might that. All those mights.

I may very well be in deep trouble at this moment but – I'm sorry – I wouldn't change a thing. My main objective, I think, in life is not to hurt anybody deliberately. Standing up and being counted is a different thing from hurting people. I'm working class, always have been. In the unlikely event of my ever reaching millionaire status, I'll still believe myself to be working class.

I had to explain to some idiot once who asked me why I was a socialist "with all your money". If only it were true. If only. I pointed out that I had to work for my living. I have no private income. If I didn't work, I would have no money coming in at all. I know what it's like to be hungry. To be cold and to be out of work. Once you've been there, you never forget it. When my critics attack me I can only shake my head and think, "silly, silly people." I spent years in poverty. I know it intimately and well. And it terrifies me. But I also believe you can pay too much for money. Putting yourself in a position where, for the exchange of money, you allow your rights to be taken away. Your rights to speak freely, to believe in something or someone.

When I left *Coronation Street* for a time in the early 1970s there were overtures to me for various things – advertising and other jobs. One particularly bright, sunny day I had a phone call. Would I go to the office of a very famous impresario? A well-known name in the film business. We met in a large, rather awesome room with wide French windows and a long conference table in the centre. At one end sat this large, portly gentleman. I sat two seats away.

He looked at me seriously for a moment and said: "Now then, Miss Phoenix. I think I could make you an enormous amount of money. Perhaps more than you've ever dreamed of. But there's one question I have to ask before we go any further. Tell me, Miss Phoenix. Would you do anything for money?"

I must admit, there was a pause. A pause of about five seconds which can seem an eternity. I was thinking and thinking hard. The answer had to be me, the real me.

"No," I said. "I would not do anything for money."

Wrong. End of conversation – and of any hopes of a vast fortune. But truly I could not do anything for money.

I know a young man who does odd jobs, gardening, whatever. He was trained in a factory and worked there for a time. But it wasn't living, he said. He decided to give up that job and the money because he never felt the fresh air on his face, he couldn't walk the green fields. He made his choice between a reasonably comfortable life and living free. He may be without some of the luxuries of life but the beauty around us is free for the taking. He hasn't got a video. His clothes aren't by Gucci or Pierre Cardin. But he's a happy man. That, I believe, is the important issue in life.

At one point in the march that day in Liverpool, the marchers and the lorry became separated. All the people walking went down the main street and the lorry cut down a parallel side street to try to reach the square before the others. We turned a corner to this long empty street. There was a police sergeant stood in the middle. As we chugged towards him, travelling at about five miles an hour, he turned and looked. And looked again in disbelief. Half a mile away there were a quarter of a million people marching. In that quiet street the policeman saw only the few of us on the lorry. Was this the whole of the unemployment march? We could almost see the pity in his face. As the lorry passed he shrugged as if to say, "That's life," and walked a few steps with us as if in comradeship.

We were still smiling wryly as we arrived at the square.

Strong socialist though I may be, politics in general today sickens me. I'm sick to death of the race for power, the contradictions, the changing of tunes. Let's have someone who is going to save the earth, not destroy it. Now it's time for the artists, the philosophers, the ecologists to get in there and do something.

I'm lucky. Through my windows I can see green fields and trees growing tall. Blue skies, or grey skies, with fluffy white clouds, or heavy storm clouds, scudding by. I can walk out on to the moors nearby and feel the wind in my hair. But elsewhere the land is being torn apart. I weep when I read about what's happening to the land we live in, the land that sustains us. Here we have the most beautiful place we could wish for. A place with fresh water, atmosphere, sun, rain, wind. We have crops, sea, fish, cattle. Everything we need, yet we are destroying it.

I remember when I was in New Zealand in 1975 flying over the cape in a small plane. I looked down and saw that the sea for miles around was all white.

"What's that?" I asked my companions.

"Oh, that. That's the aluminium factory. The sea's all polluted round there," they said. I could have screamed for the way it was all accepted, matter of factly.

The legend of Atlantis tells of the civilisation that had the secret of solar energy. They had everything they wanted. But underground there were strange deviants and dirty dealings. Someone got greedy and built one solar-energy station too many. It started off a chain of explosions and eruptions and the whole of Atlantis sank to the bottom of the sea. That's the legend and I reckon history repeats itself. That in some way the same thing will happen here.

I am one of a minority now, growing into a majority, who want to stop the stockpiling of nuclear weapons. Who want to keep the earth a beautiful and peaceful place to live. We're labelled cranks and idiots by some, when all we want is a future for ourselves and our families. We are all living in the shadow of something frightful. Something that mankind has never lived in before, and I think we are terribly brave. We go on making plans for the future and our children's future.

Like my friend Cheryl Murray. She has the most beautiful, adorable baby daughter. Cheryl told me once, soon after the baby was born, that she didn't read the newspapers any more. They only made her look at her child and wonder – what future can there be for her? That's terrifying. But you've got to have heart and you've got to have hope that the right-thinking people will come through in the end.

Thoughts of the ecology are never far from my mind. I'm valiantly struggling, attempting to write a fairy story, *Dreams From Dragon Mountain*. There is so much doom and destruction surrounding us these days, I like to escape into Never Never Land. Fairy Land. Somewhere in the bramble bushes. To the top of Dragon Mountain. My fairy story. Every time I read about another species of animal or flower or insect that has become extinct, I rush to my notebook. There on Dragon Mountain I'm trying to put every small flower, beast or butterfly which over a hundred years has disappeared from the earth.

To my surprise and delight I read some time back that dragons had been seen again, somewhere on a remote island. Komote, I think it was. I suppose I shouldn't really be delighted because they do eat people. No, really. They do eat people. Cameramen who have gone out there to photograph the dragons have mysteriously disappeared. Cameras, tripods and other equipment were found scattered, but that's all. Of the people, no trace was ever seen. The dragons are, I understand, a cross between a dinosaur and a giant lizard. To me, dragons have always been something rather special. Symbolic of all sorts of beautiful things. Gentle, wondrous creatures. One of the small characters in my book, Ben, also thinks dragons are wonderful. This is a song I wrote for him:

> If we be human beings,
> Dear God, could we not be something better,
> Something with tender, childlike eyes,
> Fingers soft like summer sighs,
> To stroke the wings of butterflies?
> Unseen antennae, trembling,
> Aware of hurts of others.
> Arms of velvet, strength to cradle
> Frightened fur and feathers.
> Vibrant sonic ears to hear
> The faintest human scream.
> A mouth of silken rose
> To kiss away
> A small world's frightened dreams.
> Hearts and minds and souls
> To do such fabled, wondrous things.
> And, maybe as an afterthought,
> Dear God, may we have wings?

Chapter Eleven

It's strange how love finds you when you're least expecting it, and least prepared. There I was, in my fifties, two failed marriages behind me, trying to pick up the threads of my life after the trauma of Alan's death. Who would think I'd be given yet another chance to find happiness?

I planned to go away with friends for a holiday in Cornwall. The annual trip with all the gang. Tony went back to stay at his mother's house.

"Will you do something for me?" he asked before he left. "Will you ring me every day?"

The cottage where we stayed was lovely. Very secluded, well away from the tourist areas. And it had no phone. I can't tell you what it cost me in ten pence pieces, ringing Tony from the nearest phone box.

On the third day of our stay there, a wonderful bunch of flowers arrived. With them was a love letter from Tony. Suddenly I realised I was missing him terribly. The ten-minute phone calls grew into an hour, an hour and a half. I couldn't wait to get home. We talked about a public appearance I had to do in Liverpool when I got back.

"I promise you I'll take you on a ferry trip across the Mersey," Tony said. "And I'm going to kiss you behind the cabin."

We never did get to go on the ferry. We were delayed

getting to Liverpool and there wasn't time. But I did get my kiss – eventually and, after several attempts.

On our first night together again Tony told me he loved me. "I love you too," I said.

We rushed into each other's arms. And missed. It was like Comic Cuts. He was still unsteady on his feet and I'm never a great one for balance. As we came to embrace Tony toppled over on to the settee and I went with him. We fell about laughing. Between us, we had to have something like half a century of theatrical experience, embracing people on stage, complete strangers. And here we were unable to get it together.

"I'll tell you what," said Tony. "I'll stand here and you come to me – but not too fast."

It was all so silly but we laughed and laughed. In some ways our love is based on laughter. Tony told me once how, while he was in hospital, he thought he'd lost his sense of humour. That for him was worse than death.

Something very funny happened one day in his room, something so funny that normally he would have roared with laughter. Instead he just looked, only half interested.

"My God. I'm losing my sense of humour." He realised with a start what had happened. "I really am in trouble. I might as well be dead if I can't see the funny side of things any more."

There were other funny happenings in hospital and Tony did laugh again. But for a while he thought it was touch and go. It taught him an important lesson which he tried to pass on to me. When he came back into my life I was finding little to laugh about. I was very far down, and trying desperately not to sink any further. With Tony I started to laugh more. I suddenly found myself laughing, really laughing. I think it was the tremendous courage he showed, the way he managed to turn the story of his time in hospital into one big joke.

Here were two very badly wounded people. Me in one way, he in another. Yet because we found great friendship before we found love, I think we got much more from each other.

Introducing Tony to my friends was hilarious. They were all heavily protective towards me. Even Peter Adamson threatened to punch him if he hurt me in any way. I got the question over and over again. "Are you sure it's not pity? We know you. You need someone who's going to look after you for a change."

There were some flippant remarks too from one particular lady. "She collects lame dogs and cripples, you know," she said. She meant to be funny. But it hurt Tony a little. They were all wrong. It certainly wasn't pity and I wasn't the one doing the looking after. Tony looks after me. He nags me too – something no one has ever done before. It's all for my own good.

I couldn't tell Tony how I felt for him. The words were all there, ready in my heart, but I couldn't get them out. I wrote them down instead, in a poem, which I never dreamed of showing him. One day in my dressing room at Granada, Tony Warren picked up the poem lying in a mass of papers and read it.

"What's this?" he asked.

"Oh, just a bit of a fairy story I'm writing," I said.

He looked at me searchingly. "It's not you know. It's much more than that." He set about trying to persuade me to show it to 'my' Tony. Eventually, he won.

I returned home one day from the studios. Tony was in the kitchen. "Here," I said. "This is for you." I gave him the poem – and ran like hell. This is that poem:

When did you love me? Or did you?
Or was it because I was there,
Within the comfort of my walls, living the way you like to
    live?

Or did some soft tendril from my heart really entwine you?
Or do you act it out, from fear of hurting me?
Or do you think, while lying softly in my arms,
Of the cavalcade of ladies that filled your days and nights?
Beautiful – exciting – wicked.
Do you still need them?

I feel sometimes like the other Iseult,
Who nursed Tristram, wounded,
While his heart longed for Iseult the Fair.

You talk of pity – you know I have none for you,
Your pride would savage me to death
If you thought that was the way of things.
Then, we are as a mirror to one another,
For I could not bear the shambling services of pity.

I pray you, do not deceive me.
All I would have given, without the reassurance of your love.
All! Except my heart which is encapsulated in silver,
Halted, by time, and waiting only for the passing Prince to
   part the thorns.

Even the dragons sleep,
Dreaming of great battles they once flew.
Small flickers of silver and gold and red fire escape their
   nostrils,
Gently, to show they only sleep and are not dead.

Are you the Prince?
Or do I dream on, consoling myself in my sleep, of a deep and
   tender love
That will last until we are both shining dust.
Can it be this way?
Or, as you pass, on your way to another adventure,
Your wounds healing in the warmth of my dreaming palace,
Do you merely touch my sleeping face, by way of thanks,

For the herbs you found beside my bed?
Comfort, security, trust and love.

And yet, you do not cheat, and lies, to you, are paltry – as
    tinsel is to gold.
It is not in you, I believe, to damage so small a dreaming child.
Could it be that, despite my lack of wit and charm,
Could you . . . need me?

Silver dragon opens an amethyst eye – and yawns.
We think we are awake,
Are loved and do love.
Be it so.
I have not time to dream again. And Princes do not often pass
    this way.

I have, throughout my life, been the subject of much gossip. I
suppose I've been provocative enough to spark the rumours
off. It was said of me in the early days that people either loved
me or hated me. There were no in-betweens. I think that's still
true today. But when Tony came into my life again I was
beginning to believe what my enemies said about me. Beginning to think that I was a total mess. Tony's laughter pulled me
back.

He laughs at the idiotic things I do in all innocence. The way
I can, without any malice in my heart whatsoever, plunge both
feet in at once by being what I call absolutely straightforward.
He laughs at the way, despite the rough passage through life
which we've both had, I still manage to maintain a sort of
ingenuousness. He's terrified of my being conned by other
people because of it. The very thing that worried my friends
about Tony at first, makes him so protective towards me.

For so long there had been no one to share with. I wanted to
show Tony all the things I loved. I told him about the places
and the people who meant so much to me. Surprisingly, he'd
never been to Cornwall.

"You must come and see for yourself," I said. "It's so beautiful. You'll fall in love with the place."

Plans were made and one bright, sunny, early May day we packed the car and set off – with me still regaling him with the wonders of Cornwall. All the way down the weather was beautiful. The birds singing and the sun shining. When we hit Cornwall, the mist started to creep in. The weather in that area at that time of year can be a little uncertain.

I wanted to show him Lamorna Cove. I had so many wonderful memories of the place and had told so many tales about it, I felt he had to see it. As we drove down to the tip of Cornwall the mist got thicker and thicker. The rain started drizzling down. We finally fought our way to the cove where there is the most beautiful hotel, a converted abbey overlooking the whole of Lamorna Cove. The mist lay like a thick blanket all around, shrouding the buildings eerily. We booked in for the night.

"Wait until the morning," I told Tony confidently. "The mist will have cleared and the view will be fantastic – the beautiful coastline and the sea."

The next morning he dashed to the window, threw back the curtains – and was faced with a blank wall of mist. He couldn't see the terrace, never mind the view.

"Er, yes. Lovely, isn't it," he said, laughing. But later he did see Lamorna Cove and other parts of Cornwall and fell in love with them as I had done.

During that same visit we decided to have lunch at the Budock Vein in Falmouth, another of the favourite places I'd been telling Tony about. It was out of season and we were late arriving. The place was deserted with only a skeleton staff to keep it ticking over. All they could provide for lunch was fish and chips. We'd travelled hundreds of miles, from the north of England to the south, to eat fish and chips. How crazy can you get. Another of those occasions which could easily have been a disaster. Another time when instead of shouting at each other, we fell about laughing.

Our first New Year together we went with friends to Robert Carrier's place in Suffolk. We flew there in a private plane and stayed nearby. The meal was wonderful, the old Hintlesham Hall a sight to see, decorated with Christmas trees and softly flickering candles. Three minutes to midnight absent-minded Annie here decides she wants to go to the loo. The facilities in the hall are sumptuous with an enormous ante-room lined with mirrors and, off that, the loos themselves. I lost track of time.

Back at the table the rest of the crowd were beginning to worry. "New Year's going to be here and we're going to bring it in without her. We'll have to go and find her."

I came out of the loo to find all the gentlemen and the other lady in our party assembled in the ladies' powder room. We brought the New Year in there, all singing, "Should old acquaintance be forgot."

The following day we were to fly back to Manchester. It dawned bright, clear and cold. As we arrived at the private airfield where the little plane was, Tony turned to me. "It's New Year's Day and I'm going to run for the first time."

He hadn't even been able to walk without pain until then, but run he did. Across the tarmac and up to the plane. The rest of us stood and watched, cheering and waving. "Come on, Tony. You can do it. Nearly there. Hooray!" You would have thought we were cheering on the winner of a marathon race. I suppose in a way that's what it was for Tony. He'd thought he'd never walk again after the accident. To run was a dream.

Tony's recovery was slow and painful. But through it all there was laughter. I think on many occasions he laughed when he really felt like crying, but after his experience in hospital when he thought his sense of humour had deserted him, he vowed he wasn't going to give in. The more I learned of his inner fight, the more I was filled with admiration and love. He told me how he had held back feeling sorry for himself.

"Oh God, what's going to become of me?" he found himself saying over and over again. It became like a twitch and he had to find some way to stop it. There was a series of exercises he had to do in hospital and everytime he said the dreaded words, or even thought them, Tony made himself go through the exercises.

"That first morning," he told me later. "I was knackered. I'd said it so many times."

There were times, of course, when the pain was too much to bear. Laughter was then impossible and Tony found his spirit leaving his body. It's a phenomenon I know other people have experienced but it only happens to those who are close to death or in a trancelike state. They do actually leave their bodies.

Tony told me he could look down on himself, watching the doctors and nurses frantically trying to force some life into his fading body. On one occasion he realised he was dying, the life-support machines were bleeping around the bed, and he made a conscious decision to return to his body. It sounds too fantastic to believe, I know, but it is true. The pain was extreme, and out of the body experiences are the true source of escape.

Tony was strung out, his hands in plastic bags on hooks so that he couldn't touch himself. He had a bell under his chin which he could press if he needed help and he was just left like that. In that situation the ability to step outside his pain-wracked body must have been an enormous release. I'm sure it was one of the things that saved his life. Tony can still do it and I'm envious of his gift.

When he left the rehabilitation centre Tony returned to his mother's house near the sea in Liverpool. He was very weak and his feet were swollen beyond recognition. He wore felt boots, size 15 on one foot and size 12 on the other. His feet are down to size eight now so you can imagine what they looked like!

One day he decided to go to the corner shop. He set off, but as he reached the corner the wind was so strong and he was so weak that he was blown backwards. It was like a scene from *The Lemon Drop Kid* with Bob Hope. He gave up and went back home. "You were quick," said his mum.

When he came to stay on the top floor of my cottage, I didn't realise what a challenge I was presenting him with. Going up two flights of stairs to his room was like climbing Everest every night before going to bed. I have pictures hanging on every conceivable bit of wall space, up the stairs, and on the landings. Tony told me only recently that it was a year before he realised there were paintings on the wall facing as you come downstairs.

"I was always looking down at the stairs and my feet, willing them to behave. One day I looked up, saw the paintings . . . and fell down the rest of the stairs."

Fortunately, or unfortunately, whichever way you look at it, most of Tony's burns were on his legs and feet and are therefore covered. Only the scars on his hands show, so that people tended to forget about them. They would come up to him, slap him on the knee by way of greeting, and wonder why Tony howled in pain. That wasn't too bad at home or with friends but imagine the reaction of others, all engaged in polite conversation at a reception or something, on hearing great roars from across the room.

Tony was always worried when that happened or when they saw him stumble that they would think him drunk. Possibly some people did. But not those who know and love Tony. They know he will never drink again. There was one occasion, however, when he must have looked for all the world like the traditional slapstick stage drunk. We had been invited to some posh opening night. There we all were dressed in our best, Tony wearing the beautiful new jacket I'd bought him as a present. The buffet was laid out on long tables and we were queuing to be served, plates in hand.

Suddenly, a woman beside us saw something she fancied on the table. She dived in between Tony and another guest. As she brushed past he was too weak to withstand the weight and, hand holding plate, he was unable to break his fall. Tony fell on to the table, his jacket sleeve right across a dish of trifle. A stifled gasp ran round the room. All eyes were on us as Tony was hauled out of the trifle. Was he drunk? No, just too weak to withstand a woman's pushing.

That jacket was fated from the first. Every time he wore it someone managed to spill something down it. Just back from the dry cleaners after its meeting with the trifle, Tony wore the jacket to another function. A lady rushed up to greet him. "Tony, wonderful to see you again," she said and promptly spilt her champagne all down his front. After a couple more mishaps, Tony got fed up with all the cleaning bills and passed the jacket on to his brother.

Chapter Twelve

I once said I hoped to grow old disgracefully. Well, I've changed my mind. I hope never to grow old, at least in my head. When people tell me they're worried about growing old, I always remember those words Gene Kelly made famous. "Don't move, don't stir. The best is yet to come." In my heart I hope I'll always be young. The rest of me is a different matter. People say to me that Elsie's looking better these days. I wouldn't agree. I think now I've caught up, if not passed, the age Mrs Tanner was supposed to be.

We had a time when the scriptwriters and directors were trying to make the story too real. In the theatre we never refer to birthdays until a person gets to be about eighty or more. In the Street the scriptwriters kept on putting in birthdays. Elsie had so many I lost track. But if you add them all on to the age she was supposed to be at the start I reckon she'd be nearly sixty now. That's ridiculous.

I play her as an indeterminate forty-five to fifty-year-old. That's the way all ladies of my age-group play it. I'm playing it like it is, a lady who's experienced, has two grown-up children and grandchildren. She once had to say the line: "Eh, Elsie. You're just about ready for the knacker's yard." I'd say she'd been there, and back. But would she leave off the make-up? Never. She has far too much bravado for that.

I'm always being told off for smoking. I make a deal with

my friends in the Street. "When they take the lead out of petrol, I'll stop smoking," I say. But I do smoke too much. I try to give it up. Every day – for ten minutes. But nothing works. I still get through sixty a day – I probably only smoke about thirty to forty of those in actual fact. The rest are wasted.

One half of me desperately wants to give up – it's a filthy habit. The other half doesn't. I enjoy smoking. I talked to a very famous hypnotist about it.

"You'll never give up," he said, "if you enjoy it." He tried hypnosis in any case. He put me under – at least everybody thought he did. I wasn't sure. "When you come out of this trance, you'll never want another cigarette as long as you live," he intoned.

I could see everybody watching me. Faces all around me, watching. Oh, my God, I thought – and promptly lit up a fag.

At least four other hypnotists have tried – and failed – to help me. As soon as they tell me: "You'll walk out of here and you'll feel sick when you have a cigarette," I can't wait to get hold of one. Which reminds me . . . I could do with one now.

I'm inclined to think it's hereditary. My dad was a very heavy smoker and my mother smoked until she was about fifty-four. Then the most amazing thing happened. She came downstairs one morning with a packet of cigarettes, and chucked them on the fire. This from a lady who used to scrabble around for cigarettes.

"What on earth . . . " I said. "What are you doing?"

"I have stopped smoking," she said loftily.

"Oh, yeah," I said. "I'll believe that when I see it."

It took a fortnight of bad temper, screaming and irritability. At the end of that fortnight she never smoked again. Never, ever smoked again. And she was a much heavier smoker than me. But despite the input of all that nicotine into my lungs I seem to have retained my vitality. And, to many people, that is enormous. In our younger days Tony and I were both full of energy and steam. We've calmed down considerably, but there's a lot of it left. Too much for some people. Years ago Tony and I would have been unbearable together for too long. There are people who think we're pretty unbearable now.

I overheard a friend say to another woman: "Oh, I think Tony's lovely."

There was a pause.

"If you ask me," said her companion, "they're ideally suited."

I guessed what she really meant.

My dear friend, Keith Pollitt, was instrumental many years ago in giving me a much needed boost. About sixteen years ago, when I was hitting the deck, head in hands exhausted with the amount of work I was doing, Keith appeared like a Fairy Godmother waving a bottle in front of me.

"Take this Cinderella," he said. "And all will be well."

"Phooey," I said. "What is it? Fortifies the over forties?"

"No. Something much better than that," he said.

Doubtfully and dubiously I took the bottle from him as if it was about to explode.

"Remember," piped Keith cheerfully. "Three times a day."

I took his tonic, liked it, found it helped enormously and have been taking it ever since. When people say: "How do you do it? How d'you keep so young?" that's the reason. My horse and dogs take Bio-Strath too, in another form, and the venerable Chips, the oldest at sixteen, is bouncing round like a pup.

Keith told me much about Dr Pestalozzi, head of the Bio-Strath Laboratories in Switzerland where the tonic is made, but only this year did I get a chance to meet him on a visit to Zurich. He's a fascinating man – a descendant of the Pestalozzi who founded the famous village for orphan children over there around the turn of the century. At his laboratories he's developed a range of herbal remedies.

Keith came with me on the trip and took me to see Dr

Brandenberger who runs the largest organic farm in Europe. The vegetables grown there, all without the use of pesticides or artificial fertilisers, are used to make Biotta juices. While we were there I met a Yorkshire lady called Sheila. Her husband had been unable to find work in England and so they had both gone over to live and work. She was delighted to find Elsie Tanner standing amongst the vines at the Biotta farm.

I'm passionately interested in herbs and herbal cures. I'm not a fanatic but I would rather take something like that which is perfectly natural than some of the 'wonder' drugs of our modern technology. I'm told that Harry Secombe and Barbara Cartland, and some famous sports personalities, take the tonic too. Perhaps that's why we're all still going strong.

Herbs aside, I think it's being involved and concerned with other people that keeps you young. My years in rep left me for the most part without bitch. That's not to say I never indulge in a female bitchy, gossipy session. But I feel horribly guilty for days after if I do. The repertory companies I worked in were all the family I had apart from my mother and we all tried to keep on happy terms. Now I like to see young people get on. And I'm interested in the new trends around me.

The cast of *Coronation Street* has a long-running joke. "We'll be here till we die," they say. "And even then, they'll still be letting in the public to view us." The other day workmen were digging a hole on the Street itself. Julie Goodyear was watching the work intently. "See those holes," she said to me. "Those are our burial plots. Yours is the deep one in the corner. Now, you can pick your stone."

"Well, I want an angel on horseback," I said, jokingly, "leading two dogs."

"They're going to let the public in to look at 'em, you know," Julie said with a huge grin. "And I bet they'll sell artificial flowers at the entrance . . . so they can collect them and sell 'em again next day."

Coronation Street is like a village and the people who work there its villagers. Like any village it has its moments of high gossip. It reacts strongly to any hint of scandal. "Did you hear . . . ?" riffles through its corridors.

With me the usual opening gambit is: "I read in last night's paper. Is it true?" Almost every day someone will open a newspaper to find a story about at least one member of the Street. "Did you really say that?" they'll ask. All too often the answer is: "No. I never gave an interview." I believe in publicity of a kind that amuses the public. The other kind of publicity I've never sought. It comes to me, I don't go to it. On one occasion, not too long ago, I was the target for one of these stories which come out of the blue. I knew nothing about it. I never gave an interview to the newspaper concerned.

I had been out to dinner with my publishers. A superb meal in warm, friendly company. The conversation touched lightly on stories that had appeared in the day's newspapers about how I had not stood during the singing of 'Land of Hope and Glory' at some function the night before.

"It was a storm in a teacup," I told my companions. "The papers blew it up out of all proportion. The night had become a little rowdy and I didn't want to join in with the boozy singing."

The conversation turned to other topics. My books, other people's books. Actors and actresses we knew. It was late when Tony and I drove up to the cottage. The lane is normally deserted at night, apart from the cars belonging to people who live nearby. But there, a short way from my house, was a strange car. Inside, two mysterious-looking people were lurking.

"Stay where you are," Tony said to me. "They could be muggers. Anybody. Stay back."

Two men got out of the car and walked towards us. Journalists, they said, from the Daily Whatever. Anticipating, or so I thought, their questions about the 'Land of Hope and Glory' story, I said a little wearily: 'Yes. It's true. I didn't stand—"

"No. It's not about that, Miss Phoenix," they said.

"Oh. Well, what—"

"It's about you leaving the Street."

"Yes," I said. "I'm going out for ten weeks to do a summer season in Bournemouth."

"No. It's not about that either," they said gravely. "This is serious. It's all over tomorrow's front page of a certain newspaper. About how you're demanding a film star's salary and threatening to leave *Coronation Street*."

"What? I never said anything," I told them. I was flabbergasted. I thought it must be a joke. "It's not true. It's all rubbish," I said, walking inside the cottage.

The next morning, early, very early, the phone started ringing and kept on ringing. My friend Tony Warren was one of the first callers.

"Hello, Pat," he said. "It's not true, is it?"

"What?" I asked sleepily.

"The story in the paper. About you leaving the Street."

The reporters had been telling me the truth. It wasn't a joke. "No, it isn't true," I said. "Of course it isn't. You know me better than that. I never even gave the paper an interview."

"Oh, good," said Tony, the relief apparent in his voice. "I knew it didn't really sound like you."

After a hectic couple of hours when the phone never seemed to stop ringing, I managed to get into work. Minutes later my boss Bill Podmore came tearing into my dressing room, waving a newspaper at me. "You might have had the courtesy to tell me first if you're leaving. Have you seen—"

"But . . . But I'm not," I said, managing at last to get a word in edgeways. "The first thing I knew about it was this morning. When my phone started ringing."

Everybody, whatever their job, grumbles at some time

about work. We're lucky to be able to. I'm constantly in my 'beard' about this, that and t'other. My usual grouse is that I'm under-employed. I'm a workaholic. I've been heard to mutter darkly for years: "It's no good. I haven't got enough to do. I can't go on like this."

There's my annual – sometimes even monthly – trip up the stairs. Bending my boss's ear: "I can't stand this script. I need more to do." Bill must be thoroughly fed up with it by now. It's a well-known speech of mine, oft delivered within the portals of Granada. Nobody takes a blind bit of notice. I've done it now since 1962, every year at least, regularly.

But within Granada. Never outside. When the furore had died down – giving way, I might add, to great hoots of laughter and new gags, "Leaving again then, eh, Pat?" – I sidled up to Bill. In an exaggerated aside I said: "Well, if I never told the papers, who did? I've been saying it for years to you. Are you the mole? Eh, Bill. Did you leak it?"

I had to skip smartly out of his range. Bill went puce. He looked about to blow up again . . . and then burst out laughing. In spite of the laughs, the article did hurt me. The bit about the money especially. I'm not a greedy lady. We all need money, yes, but I'm not money-orientated. I like to work for my money. I like to earn it. That's the reason behind my grumbles. If I'm not doing a lot, if I'm not working very hard, I don't feel I am earning it.

And, to be truthful, I'm daft with money. It's a great joke amongst my friends. If I have 20p, I don't have it for more than ten minutes. I'm very likely to give it away. If I had a million, it would be the same.

Chapter Thirteen

Elsie Tanner has brought me many things – some of them good, others not so good. One of the better aspects has been the chance to travel, to visit places I might otherwise never have seen. But I think I would have travelled anyway, somehow or other. It's the gypsy in me. If I hadn't succeeded in my acting career I would probably have gone about with a donkey like Robert Louis Stevenson. Instead, I've travelled the world by jet, by ship, even, in part, by taxi.

I was holidaying in Djerba with friends. The plan was to fly to Tunis to spend the last few days there before catching the flight home. On the last day on the island I came down with a terrible stomach bug. There was no way I could get on that plane. My friends flew off for three days of fun while Bill Nadin stayed behind with me. But I knew that somehow I had to get to the mainland to catch that flight. I had to be back on the Street. Was there any other way back to the mainland, we asked? "Well, yes," the locals replied. "By taxi."

Djerba is an island joined to North Africa by a road across the sands. The journey from there to Tunis takes about a day driving. So we got into the taxi and set off, me clutching a bottle of soda water and a packet of dry biscuits. It took us right through the Western Desert – a most extraordinary trip. Miles and miles of sand, broken by the occasional small village, the shells of crashed airplanes and abandoned tanks and finally, El Djem, the little village where the Roman amphitheatre is.

There is a piece out of it like a slice of cake where a local Arab prince took some of the stone for building. Fortunately, he took a very neat slice which now enables you, if you're passing, to see right inside this perfectly preserved amphitheatre. It was an experience I would never have had if it had not been for that stomach bug. We finally caught up with the rest of the party in Tunis. They'd had a terrible time, an awful hotel, and we'd had a most wonderful day's drive, arriving in good time to catch the plane home.

The plane home caused problems for me on another trip, a working holiday in Singapore. Johnny Briggs, Anne Kirkbride, Bill Podmore and I were taken over there several years ago by the *TV Times* who wanted to do a feature on the Street abroad. Waiting in the crowded airport lounge for our flight home, we were told there would be a delay. Quite how long we didn't realise. A plane had crashed into the runway and the airport staff were busy rebuilding the tarmac. They kept on making apologies for the delay. We would be leaving soon, they assured us every time. Finally, at about one o'clock in the morning – we should have taken off at eight the previous evening – we were ushered on to the plane. Great, we thought, we're on our way.

We weren't. We sat on that stinking hot plane until daylight. They were still building the runway. The whole delay was about eighteen hours. That was a terrible ending to an otherwise wonderful trip. Wonderful, but hard work. The *TV Times* photographers kept us on the go most of the time. As ever, when any of the Street get together, we had a lot of fun too.

Anne Kirkbride made me laugh. There we were in the most beautiful surroundings. Lovely swimming pools, oriental gardens, fabulous scenery. A place full of divine delights and

The day the Queen came down our *Street*. She's pictured here with Sir Denis Forman, Chairman of Granada, during her visit to the new set in 1982.

Exercise for Tony – and a little gentle sketching for me. A rare day off spent in the quiet of the conservatory at my cottage. (© *Sunday Mirror*, Manchester.)

Tony and I share a love of music, and in our rare quiet moments we gather round the piano at the cottage for a good singsong. (© *Sunday Mirror*, Manchester.)

Opposite, top: Midnight ... and another New Year begins. That's me in party mood at my cottage.

Opposite, bottom: The side of things *Coronation Street* viewers don't see. With all those cameras, cables and overhead microphones crammed into the studio set of the Rovers, it's surprising there's any room left for the actors!

Opposite, top: "Win the race, and I'll marry you," I told my racehorse, Lymond, at Thirsk in spring '83. Me and my big mouth ... he won it, of course! (© Photosport, Aughton, Lancashire.)

Opposite, bottom: A pint in the Rovers for Dustin Hoffman when he visited the *Coronation Street* set in 1983. A super guy – Elsie and I both fell for him.

Below: I love collecting paintings, and every one of them has a story to tell. There's hardly a spare inch of wall space in my cottage. (© *Sunday Mirror*, Manchester.)

Above: Good reason to celebrate. With all the changes that have taken place on *Coronation Street*, there are still a few old familiar faces left. Bill Roache, Doris Speed, Jack Howarth and me in the Rovers earlier this year (1983).

Left: Tony and I with Dr Fred Pestalozzi and his English wife, Sylvia, in their garden overlooking Lake Zurich – a picture take during our visit to the Bio-Strath laboratories in Switzerland in spring '83.

Relaxing at my health club.

Glamour girl – what me? The soft lighting at my health club does wonders for a woman.

Anne was busy telling me she'd had a letter from home and "the plumber's been to fix the pipes, but the joiner still has to come and do the cupboard door." She couldn't understand why I was laughing.

She created quite a stir in Singapore. Now, without those Deirdre specs, Annie is a very pretty girl with a super figure. She always goes braless. One day she was walking in her high heels past a building site where there were hundreds of Singapore men working. As she walked everything was bouncing. The whole site stopped work to watch Annie go by. How to hold up production!

Anne is great fun but she has a temper too. The photographers wanted to take pictures of us both in cheong sams, the native dress. So there we were all dressed up in this full oriental gear and the photographers dragging us all round Singapore looking for the right location. Suddenly Anne turned on them. "If you think I'm bloody well trailing all the way round Singapore in this bloody outfit, you've got another think coming."

Johnny Briggs and I also had a little altercation over something while we were there and he was sulking. I had to do something to pull him out of it. I went out shopping and I found a marvellous T-shirt with 'I used to be conceited but now I'm perfect' printed across the front. He nearly died laughing when he saw it.

On that trip I tasted my first Singapore Sling in the bar of Raffles. Johnny took a picture of me sitting alone at the bar with my drink, looking very sultry in an off-the-shoulder dress. He calls it his Shanghai Lil.

Boogie Street was also an eye-opener. It's the street of a thousand ladies but most of the girls are boys. Bill Podmore and I were like peasants up from the country, staring at them. We couldn't tell which were which. Bill had his pocket picked by one of them. The photographers wanted to take a picture of him with a so-called girl. He was sat there with his legs crossed and 'she' had her arm around him. He had tight trousers on and his money was deep in his pocket, trapped there, he thought, by the way his leg was bent. He was wrong. 'She' got his money somehow.

If Singapore was a wonderland, Bangkok was paradise. I first saw it on the way to somewhere else when we landed at the airport to refuel. We were allowed off the plane into the airport buildings. As I came down the steps I saw the jungle encroaching as it does on the runways. There were fish ponds and bridges all round and people were selling rubies and diamonds; jade for a few pounds. I was enchanted and decided then to return. I've been back several times.

For stopovers on long flights to Australia or wherever, everyone goes to Fiji, the isle of guano. When Alan and I got the chance to tour in New Zealand, I said I wanted to stop over in Bangkok for a couple of weeks. We stayed at the International Hotel, a black and gold pagoda with two enormous foo dogs at the entrance, and standing in its own grounds which were populated by a menagerie of wild birds and animals.

The people of Bangkok are a delight and a joy to see. Beautiful little people who greet you with fragrant frangipani flowers or try to sell you dirty postcards and ripe bananas at the same time. The city is so alive. On every street corner there is a wot, a little temple for the spirits of ancestors. Every time the people pass one they bow. You can imagine in that teeming traffic, driving along and suddenly your driver mutters something unintelligible and gets up to bow to a wot he's just passed. It makes for interesting journeys.

Alan was in the middle of one of his benders at this time so I was left on my own quite a lot. And I didn't want to miss anything. On one of these occasions I met the boys from MASH – the real soldiers not the actors. They had come out of the jungle on leave. Most of them were American but one had done a degree at Manchester University and had seen *Coronation Street* and recognised me. We talked a lot and became great mates.

They asked me to go with them to a fabulous beach there, a stretch of white coral sand with one hotel and a few beach huts underneath coconut trees. Pure enchantment, it sounded to me. I didn't go but I was tempted. I don't think Alan would have missed me. Not for two or three days – such was the state of affairs then. We did go on a boat down the muddy, yellow river, bordered on both sides by steaming jungle. As we got further downriver I said: "Oh, look, fireworks."

"Don't be bloody stupid," the others replied. "It's the fighting down there."

At the end of the two weeks we flew to New Zealand and yet another culture shock. Arriving there is like stepping back in time. At the airport some wag has written on the wall: "You are now arriving in Wellington. Please put your watches back fifty years." Well, yes, it is like that but I love it. There are still manners, consideration, and people form communities. I love the people, their warmth and generosity. It's a divine place.

I got very fat visiting their pancake parlours where they served enormous pancakes layered with all sorts of fruits and ice cream. But there was plenty of exercise too. In a speed boat I travelled three hundred miles down the Wanganui River; an exciting trip at tremendous speeds.

I can also claim to have played snowballs on the top of Mount Cook. To get there we'd travelled in a snow plane, flying through Cinnerama Gap. That's an opening between the very high mountains through which, on a clear day, a small plane can fly with only six inches to spare on either side. We were all muffled up in overcoats against the snow. But when we landed on Mount Cook and got out into thick crumbly snow the weather was boiling hot, the sun belting down. Beautiful. And up there we had a snowball fight.

While Alan and I were in New Zealand I was made a Maori princess. The ceremony was at a hangi an outdoor feast where they bury all the food wrapped in white cloths in the ground near to the hot springs. There it cooks slowly. A beautiful Maori chief wearing traditional garb was addressing the crowd in a deep, ferocious voice. They called him Uncle Tom.

He beckoned me to join him on the pile of stones by a hot spring on which he was standing. "This is my great friend, Miss Elsie Tanner from Eeng-land," he boomed. Then he turned to me and in the highest, sweetest voice imaginable said: "I think we'd better get off, dear, it's going to blow." What a comedown. Maori warriors crowded around, threatening me with their maris – the traditional green stone club. Then they rubbed noses with me, garlanded me with flowers and gave me a tiki – a little green-stone carving which is meant to represent my spirit.

Years later I made a great impression on the people of Canada too, though not quite the one I'd intended. We were there to tour with *My Cousin Rachel* – Ernst, McDonald Hobley, Donald McIver, myself and the rest of the company. The weather was bitterly cold, snowing heavily most of the time we were there. The small plane in which we travelled from town to town was constantly tossed and buffeted by the wind.

The company always carried its own bar. A few bottles of spirits – no mixers – in a paper bag. It was with us this particular day as we waited to board the plane for our next journey. The weather was terrible – and steadily getting worse. It turned into a blizzard and the pilot announced he could not fly that day. The rest of the journey, another hundred miles, had to be by bus.

A few miles on, the boys were getting very bored. "Open up the bar," one of them said. "Come on, let's have a drink to cheer things up." They all got well into the booze.

We arrived at our destination and off the bus piled about

seventy-eight suitcases, Miss Phoenix, Mr Walder, another three young men carrying the prostrate leading man Donald McIver, and another one behind carrying his boots.

"Miss Phoenix's entourage?" the hotel receptionist asked.

Well, yes, I suppose you could call it that, although I'm not usually followed by the corpse of Hamlet and his boots.

"Put all this," she directed with a wave of the hand, "in Miss Phoenix's room." Which meant my drunken friend Donald, the boots, the suitcases and all the other actors. What an entrance.

Donald McIver and I became great friends. A lovely guy, he taught me a lot about life. I hope I taught him something of my philosophy too.

I've visited and worked in so many parts of the world yet, sad to say, I don't know the village where I live nearly well enough. It's one of the problems of my work. When I'm here, I'm at the studio most of the time, coming home at night too tired to think about exploring. When I'm on holiday I need to get away completely. Somewhere where I can relax and be myself. I have two places of retreat which I love – Cornwall and Yugoslavia. In Yugoslavia I can explore or laze in the sun as I please, going completely incognito. Or so I thought.

Last year Tony and I went to Sveti Stevan, a place I've been to many times, but for Tony it was his first visit. They don't get English television out there but somehow the authorities had heard I was some sort of TV personality.

We landed at Dubrovnik to be met by two officials, a man bearing a great bunch of gladioli and two men wearing dark glasses who appeared to be secret service.

"Who are they?" I asked Tony. The party walked towards us. They were waiting for me. The man with the gladioli spoke first. "We hear zat you are a great television star. Welcome to our country." He handed me the flowers.

"This television," one of the others asked, "is like *Dallas*? Is very rich?"

"No, not very rich. Very poor," I tried to explain.

"Ah, good. Dobra, dobra."

During the course of this interview I couldn't help looking at the two impassive gentlemen in dark glasses. They hadn't spoken, hadn't moved.

"Who are they?" I asked, pointing at the two dark-suited men.

"Is security."

"Well, don't they ever smile?"

There was a quick, huddled conversation. Then the two security men turned to me with the tiniest, sickliest of smiles. I fell about laughing and eventually made them laugh too.

The people were wonderful to us. Tony was still very weak and in some pain but he managed to swim which is good exercise for him. It was the first time he had unashamedly gone into the sea. We became very friendly with some of the local boys who showed great interest and compassion over his burns. They told us about a doctor who lived up there, who had developed a special burn cream. One of the Yugoslav film stars had burnt her face terribly in an accident, and friends had managed to get her up to the doctor straight away. She is without scars, they said, because of the great doctor's cream.

Yugoslavia is, to me, one of the few places that still remains fairly unspoilt. It does have its tourist trade but I try to go to the furthest parts, on the Albanian border.

There are parts of Cornwall which are still unspoilt too. I think it's a country all on its own. The Cornish believe visitors should have passports to cross the River Tamar. I agree – it's almost another world. The pace of life slows down and the people are so special – all the artists, the sculptors, the people who have dropped out. The fishermen, the people who were born there and work so hard.

I have some very dear friends in Cornwall and many beautiful things to remind me of them. My home is full of them – paintings, sculptures, books, even a little treasure from the bottom of the sea. Treasure I could have had more of if I'd followed my heart and not my head.

One gloomy, dismal day my old friend, Roland Morris, rang, with sunshine in his voice. He's a man of many roles – former diver, marine salvage operator, artist, writer, restaurateur and treasure hunter.

"Do you want to buy into a treasure, m'dear?" he asked. "I'm going after the wreck of the *Association*."

"Give over, Roland," I said, incredulously.

"You can buy into the treasure for £500."

Well, I ask you. What would you do? I said no.

The *Association* was one of four ships which went on the rocks around the Scilly Islands in 1707. As the flagship, she was carrying much of the bounty taken from enemy ships some months before. The twenty-one ships of the line were led by the *Association* and her Admiral Sir Cloudesley Shovell, who was a bit of a twit I should think. Sailing home to England, he became lost. Blithely the others followed him. A wrong decision by the Admiral turned them into the path of the treacherous Gilstone Ledges. Some managed to escape, but four ships hit the rocks. Almost two thousand men went down with the treasure.

Roland had a chart showing the *Association* wreck and had actually seen the bare bones of the ship at calm water. His eyes were set on the treasure of bronze cannons, silver and gold hidden below.

I didn't hear any more about it for some time until I turned on the radio one morning and heard the announcer say: " . . . And the divers are literally walking on carpets of silver and gold."

Roland had found his treasure. The divers had located the

cannons and while securing the tackle to bring them to the surface, one of the men saw a flash of gold. A golden Lois lay at his feet. He looked to his left and saw another. And another, and another. The trail of gold led the divers to a tiny opening in the tumbled rocks, so small they had to take off their oxygen bottles before they could swim into it. Inside the cave was most of the treasure of the *Association*.

Roland gave me a piece of eight, and a sword hilt, to remind me of what I'd missed.

I was very grateful to him in the days after Alan's death. I was still down in Cornwall and the press were hounding me. Everywhere I went there were three cars following. Roland owns the Admiral Benbow restaurant and one day when the trailing of the reporters and photographers became too much to bear, we met him there. He sneaked us through back streets and secret passageways, turning here, darting down an alley-way there, until we came out in his flat. Outside the press were searching up and down the main street, looking for me. He sent his spies out later to see if the coast was clear to make our getaway. Roland's knowledge of the smugglers' alleyways gave us at least one day's peace.

I have many pictures from Cornwall on my walls but one in particular is very dear to me. It's a first proof copy of a painting by Ronnie Copas. It's of St Francis and the Wildfowl and was specially commissioned by the Wildfowl Trust and counter-signed by Sir Peter Scott. It has its own special story.

I first met Ronnie Copas playing a guitar in a hotel at Marazion. He said he was an artist and lived in a castle on a beach. He invited us there for tea. He actually did live in the turret of a ruined castle for which he paid the local council five bob a week. He said he was trying to get a council house.

We arrived there at sunset and the still slightly wet beach glowed pink in its light. There were two naked blonde chil-dren skipping and laughing, with the wind whipping through their hair, a pretty girl in a long skirt and Ronnie, who looks like a young gypsy. It was a perfect picture.

We walked up to the turret, up past ruined sections of the castle. Ronnie painted hundreds of pictures of yachts out at sea – tourists' pictures – just to make money to keep the family. I'd seen them, and many others like them, before. He took me into another room and showed me the most beautiful paintings done in the time-honoured way, with hand-mixed paints and great skill. He gave me a couple of small pictures.

Later, when he was down on hard times, he wrote to me asking if I would buy a particular painting for £100. It was an exceptional work of art, worth far more than £100. I sent him the money and wouldn't take the painting. I would have considered myself totally criminal if I had taken it, and lived in guilt for the rest of my life. Ronnie Copas struggled on, perfecting his art. Eventually it was recognised and he began to get commissions. My picture of St Francis is Ronnie's way of saying thank you.

The artist Ben Maile is also a friend and he sold his first two paintings to – guess who? I walked into a gift shop in Looe and saw these two pictures.

"Oh, those are nice."

"They're very dear, Miss Phoenix," said the woman in the shop. "They're £45 each."

"I'll have 'em both," I said.

I didn't think any more about it. I brought the pictures home, hung them on my wall and loved them. Ben Maile became famous. Then up in Newcastle one time I walked into a shop. It was his studio and the cheerful, jolly man who came out was Ben Maile.

He walked over to me, smiling broadly. "You changed my luck," he said. "You bought my first two paintings."

When I thought I'd have to sell some of my paintings to keep the taxman happy, I couldn't do it. I'd rather do anything than that. Each one has a story attached to it. They're people to me, not collector's pieces.

I have so many friends in Cornwall. There's Charles Neave-Hill, the former Master of Land's End, now in America. I met him at Land's End years ago. I was with Kitty buying the books and photographs of the place – Kitty's absolutely besotted with it – when I saw this rather distinguished young gentleman approaching us.

"Hello, Miss Phoenix," he said. "How lovely to see you at Land's End. I've always been a great admirer of your work."

He asked us both to his house for dinner. He doesn't really mean it, I thought to myself. He's asking out of politeness. So we didn't go.

Later I met this great lady, who turned out to be Charles's housekeeper, Nora, a Scot. "You're a right disappointment to our Charles," she said.

"Why?" I asked.

"We had a lovely dinner table laid for you. Everything. Flowers, the lot. And ye never turned up. Oh, yes. You were a great disappointment. He's a great admirer of yours," she said.

I felt so ashamed. I really hadn't thought he meant the invitation. I dashed up to his home to make my apologies. After that we became good friends. He rings me up from all sorts of places. Florida at Christmas, Paris at New Year, Crete in the spring. You never know where he's ringing from. He's always entertaining and vastly amusing – the calls go on for twenty-five minutes.

"Charles, this must be costing a fortune," I'll say. "Where are you ringing from?" He sounds just round the corner.

"Oh, Crete," he replies nonchalantly.

He's sorely missed. A super friend, a perfect gentleman.

I remember one time Charles came north to visit. He'd never been to a sit-down fish and chip shop so Peter Dudley and I decided to take him to Mother Hubbard's in Oldham.

First we called in to an exhibition in Manchester of paintings by the artist husband of a rather eccentric, colourful London lady.

She spotted us and crossed the gallery. "Where are you going afterwards, darlings?" she drawled.

We explained our plan.

"That sounds divine. Can we join you?" she asked.

"Yes, why not." We thought she meant her and her husband. We left – with a crate of champagne as the restaurant wasn't licensed – and they agreed to join us later.

That evening the lady made her entrance – followed by about twelve other people. She had a black cloche hat on with a great pink flower on it, and a black dress split to her thigh and cut almost as low at the front. Attached was some sort of strange cerise trail. She plonked herself down next to Charles. Now this particular lady has a reputation for being outrageous. Halfway through the main course her left bosom popped out of her dress. I dropped my napkin and Peter, who was sitting next to me, did too. We had hysterics under the table.

"Have you seen it?" we giggled into our napkins.

Back up we came. Then I saw Charles pick up a table mat and hold it in front of the lady's face. I could see he was trying manfully to continue the polite conversation. What the hell's going on now, I thought.

Apparently, she'd turned to Charles and said: "Oh, these bloody fishbones. They get right under my teeth." And promptly taken out her bottom set and dropped it in her champagne glass, twirling it round with her finger.

Charles, being the perfect gentleman, had carried on talking as if nothing had happened, " . . . and what did your husband do then? Yes, I've always found the South of France absolutely interesting." All the while the teeth were swirling in the champagne glass in front of him.

Once again, Peter dropped his napkin and he and I were

under the table giggling like a couple of kids.

At the end of the meal as I, playing the perfect hostess, am showing her to the door, out popped the right bosom. The waiters and waitresses at Mother Hubbard's weren't exactly used to that sort of carry-on. I smiled thinly at them. "She loves a party," and shoved her out through the door.

Charles was speechless with shock. "Well, I say . . . I mean to say. Well, really!"

Once again Peter Dudley and I were under the table, muffling our giggles with our napkins.

The lady is really quite adorable and great fun. Certainly never boring company.

There are other great friends from Cornwall. There's Derek Tangye who writes books about Minack. He was PR at the Savoy and dropped out with his wife Jenny to write and grow flowers on the Cornish cliffs. There's the gemmologist who used to be a computer expert. He gave me a piece of fool's gold shaped in a perfect cube. The diver who's building his own house in the village where we usually stay. The lady I always buy my woollies from. She shears her own sheep, spins and knits the wool beautifully. I always find time for a visit to her farmhouse when we go down.

And there's my lovely Winnie Matthews whose cottage we sometimes stay in. Winnie has a goat called Geoffrey. No one wants billy goats in Cornwall, they're too much of a nuisance. But Winnie has a heart of gold, saw Geoffrey wandering about and took him in. He used to kick up hell but she loved him. She even went round every vet in the area to find the right one to castrate Geoffrey. It's an operation that does quieten billy goats but it can be dangerous. Winnie sent me a card at Christmas. "Geoffrey's had his operation and he's much better now," she wrote.

I'd see her in the evening, taking Geoffrey on a lead for his late walk. She has the lovely Cornish accent, and Tony once referred to her as a real Cornishwoman.

"I'm no Cornishwoman," she said. "My people came here from Cheshire in 1068. We were on the losing side at Hastings."

It does take a long time to be accepted in Cornwall but I'm lucky to be thought of as part of them. People tell me off if I haven't been down there for a while. When I was in rep, Cornwall was a place I always dreamed of going to but never had the chance. I was either working too hard or had no money. Soon after I joined the Street my friend Bill Nadin promised he would take me.

The first place I ever saw was Lamorna Cove. We arrived there late one night, turning off the road to Land's End on to a beautiful wooded track. We drove on up a steep hill and there, standing on the cliff, was a small abbey, converted into a hotel, where we stayed the night. During the rest of the week in Cornwall the people were smashing to me. They recognised me from having watched *Coronation Street* but accepted me nevertheless, without fuss or bother.

I used to have a house down there, but the taxman changed all that. It would be my dream to have a place there again, a place where I could escape to, perhaps for six months of the year – acting would be very hard to give up completely. I love the people. The dreamers and the drop-outs, the fishermen and the workers. They are an integral part of my life. Much more interesting than all this flitting about in theatrical circles. They're real.

It seems now I have friends in every quarter of the globe. Lovely Mo Fenick in Malta with his beautiful Paradise Hotel, whom I long to see again one day; Lorette Lee, the cultural leader of Manchester's Chinatown. All the friends I met in Bangkok, in Canada, Australia, New Zealand, Yugoslavia, Malta, Gibraltar, Spain, Italy, Ireland and every part of Britain. I value them all dearly.

My closest friends are a down-to-earth lot. They're not famous faces, or famous names. Kitty, my housekeeper, is possibly the most down-to-earth of them all. There's no standing on ceremony with Kitty. The few actors and actresses who do come to the house are treated just like everyone else.

"Hello, chuck," she says. "Sit down and have a cup o'tea."

When my producer rings up she's just the same. "Hello. Is that young Billy? Eee, my favourite lad." There's just no stopping her.

The only thing which does impress Kitty is royalty. The day the Queen came to the Street and I shook hands with her, Kitty thought I was wonderful. But only, as I soon realised, because I'd shaken hands with the Queen.

She's been with me now about eleven years, through the good times and the bad. She arrived a couple of days after my marriage to Alan, when I was suffering severe lung congestion and needed help in the house. The vicar who had married us came to see me.

"You don't know anyone who could help, do you?" I asked.

"Well, yes," he said. "There's a lady who works in the chapel. I'll ask her."

I was still in bed when I interviewed Kitty. She walked in, took one look at the dogs and fell in love with them. She's absolutely devoted to the animals. That's a full-time job in itself, just looking after all the birds and the dogs and the fish.

Kitty's no longer a young woman. She's seventy-five now. But she's great fun to be with. She's got a marvellous sense of humour. One trick she has, which is a hoot to everybody in the household, is her telephone voice. When the phone rings she loses her lovely north country accent.

"Hello," she'll say in her poshest voice.

"Now listen Pat—" the caller says, mistaking Kitty for me.

"This is not Pat. This is Miss Phoenix's 'ousekeeper."

She was talking one day in the kitchen. "You know, there's

three things I want to do before I die. I want to go to the Cup Final. I want to go to the Test Match. And I want to fly on Concorde." We took her to the Test Match – and it was rained off – so we set our minds on fulfilling the other two.

I have a friend in the travel business, Roy, a super bloke and extremely generous. He knew about Kitty's wish. "If you really want her to go on Concorde," he said, "I can arrange it. I'll look after the tickets from Manchester to London and you can do the Concorde bit."

We agreed and we told Kitty she was going for a trip on the Thames.

"Aren't you coming with me?" she asked.

"No. I can't get the time," I told her. I couldn't say that I wasn't able to afford it! "But I want you to get all dressed up and you'll have a good time."

Someone tipped off the press and when we got to Ringway Airport there were all the photographers, waiting. And there's Kitty, all dressed in her best, with a bunch of flowers in her arms, getting the VIP treatment.

Roy met her in London. "Do you know where you're going, Kitty?" he asked.

"No, not really."

"On Concorde. Come on, it's all arranged."

Kitty was whisked up to the super plane so quickly she didn't have time to think or speak. She's stuffed on Concorde, all on her own, given a special VIP bottle of port and spoilt rotten. The flight took her round the Bay of Biscay and back to London where Roy met her again.

"Well, Kitty. Did you enjoy it?" he asked. She was still flying and could only nod her agreement.

Then they went to lovely Beryl Reid's for tea on the Thames before Kitty boarded the plane back to Manchester.

For two days she couldn't speak. We couldn't get anything out of her other than: "Eee, I can't believe it. I can't believe it."

"Well. Did you have a good time?" we asked her.

"Lovely," she breathed.

"What was it like?"

"Eee, I can't believe it."

That went on for two days. Suddenly she came back to earth with a bang and couldn't stop talking about the trip.

I love to give surprises. For me to give pleasure to other people is my selfishness and my delight. I adore to see joy and surprise on another person's face. In this case it was better than me going, seeing the sheer delight on Kitty's face. I probably wouldn't have appreciated it.

We haven't managed the Cup Final yet. That's to come.

Nell Hayward is another friend I've known for years. She was a great theatre addict and I met her about forty years ago when I was playing in Bradford. She had a friend in the company, Jean Kitson, and used to come backstage to see her. Nell is a wonderful seamstress and she made herself very helpful to all of us in the company. She's still doing it for all of us in this house. I moved on but we kept in contact. She's a great letter writer. One of those people I thank God for, because I'm not a good correspondent. It doesn't mean to say I don't think of my friends. I do. I hold them in great respect. But every waking moment of my life is filled. When I sleep, I crash.

I become, perhaps, careless. People say to me accusingly: "You never wrote to me. You never telephone." True. If they lived a week with me they would understand why. Nell does understand. She comes to stay often and she knows when I'm worried, got things on my mind and inclined to be slightly irritable. She understands all that. There are times when I do get up everybody's back in this household. Everybody. Those are the days when I'm referred to as 'She' – She who must be obeyed. "She is being impossible. Madam is at it again."

They're all part of the family. There's Cousin Ivy too. She

has been extremely ill this year and gone bravely through all
sorts of terrible things. She's been so brave about it all, and she
has my admiration. I have very happy memories of times with
her on holiday. Peter Dudley used to tease her unmercifully.
One day in particular I remember. We were sitting in the quiet
lounge of a rather smart hotel. There were people all around.
Suddenly, Peter went into his act.

"Are you all right, mother?" he shouted down her ear. "Did
you tell her to put her hearing aid in?" he asked me, in a voice
loud enough for the people in the next hotel to hear. "Can you
hear me?" he shouted again. "Are you all right, mother?"

Cousin Ivy picked up the joke. "Eh?" she said, cupping her
hand round her ear. "What d'you say?"

The whole lounge full of people looked on, thinking she's
deaf and daft with it.

People come to my door at the strangest times. People asking
for autographs, for money, a place to stay or the party they feel
sure must be going on inside. I try to help some, others I have
to send on their way, as gently as possible.

I had no idea what to expect one day several years ago when
I answered a knock at the door. There stood a young blonde
girl, her arms full of puppy and her eyes full of tears. "Please,
miss, she's going to be shot. She's a Scottie," she sobbed.

Nothing less like a Scottie have I ever seen.

Kitty had come to the door behind me and heard the girl's
sad tale. She began to cry too. "You can't let her be killed."

What could I do with two sobbing females, one on either
side of me? The little girl, with the all-seeing eyes of a child,
knew she was on a winner.

"Oh, bring it in," I said, resignedly.

That was how Sally came into my life. She was one of an
unwanted litter of puppies that a local farmer had to get rid of.
She had been born under a tractor, judging by her condition

when she first came into the house. She stank of diesel oil, her eyes were bald and red-rimmed and she had all the signs of suffering from rickets. She looked a frightened, miserable bundle. She's in great shape now but she can still turn on that big-eyed, terrified look to order. Sal's a professional coward and uses it to her own ends. In this house no one's allowed to shout at her.

There have always been animals in my life, always will be. My life would be, perhaps, more orderly without them, but I don't think it would be very happy. They are as important to me as human beings. Little souls I care for and it's my responsibility to see they are well looked after. And for that I have to thank Kitty. I'm very lucky to have her. She adores the animals. I think she's fonder of them than she is of me. But without Kitty I couldn't function. I have to be away from home so often, I couldn't bear to think they weren't in the care of someone as kind-hearted as her.

Sally is one of five dogs in the family at the moment, the others being pekes, of some description or other. The middle two, Sophie and Sam, may not have the finest pedigrees in the world, but as soon as I saw them I couldn't resist them. I found them in a house advertising pekinese puppies for sale. The owner produced these two bedraggled little creatures. Poor little things. I had to buy them, didn't I?

Sam had asthma and a deformed ribcage and Sophie was in danger of losing her sight altogether because her eyelashes had been allowed to grow inwards. Those two have cost me a fortune in veterinary bills ever since. The baby of the family is Scott, named after F. Scott Fitzgerald. He's a tomboy, a monster who keeps tripping everyone up, forgetting he's only a little peke. Fortunately, the postman and the milkman are used to Scott now. Given half the chance he'll bite, a habit he certainly hasn't picked up from the others. He's incredibly strong for a peke and tries to do the most amazing acrobatic feats for a short-legged dog. His party piece is to jump on the wall outside the house and down the other side, something none of the other dogs, not even Sally, can do.

Bleak Holt – the animal sanctuary in Ramsbottom, Lancashire, that I try to help whenever I can – gave him to me for my birthday three years ago. He was one of a litter that had been turned out and rescued by Bleak Holt. One of the girls in wardrobe at Granada, Vera, has Scott's brother, Hammie. When he arrived here he was a right tearaway compared to my other comparatively coddled creatures. Scott was as tough as old boots, still is, running almost wild up at Bleak Holt.

That place is well named, sitting up on the moors as it does. A wonderful place and wonderful people who run it. They save ponies that have been badly treated, cats, dogs – they'll take in anything. Once they even took in a cow and a calf from a lady who wrote to me. She had to give up her farm and her pets, which included a cow called Vanity and her calf.

"It would break my heart if they had to go to the slaughterhouse," she wrote. I felt the same way too and asked Bleak Holt if they could help. They did and Vanity and child lived up there happily ever after.

Chips, however, the venerable gentleman of the family at sixteen, was a perfect specimen. He and his sister, Bossy Knickers, came from a very good kennels in Birmingham and were real show dogs. Bossy Knickers was also well-named – she bossed the whole household, humans and canines alike. She used to lead Blackie, not a dog but a wolf given to me by a zoo, into the most terrible trouble. He with his vast bulk was bound to do some damage, while Bossy would turn away at the last minute as if to say: "Nothing to do with me." She died with a cold – she sneezed and haemorrhaged in a second – and is buried in the garden along with my other sadly missed pals, Blackie and Happy Joe, each with a blood-red rhododendron over their graves. The flowers bloom now where before nothing grew.

Chips now runs the house. He is an old mate from way back who shares many memories and raids my mind.

With five dogs, walks can either be great fun or a nightmare. Chips and Sally are a perfect lady and gent. They will walk off the lead and come back when called. The others are off, trying to attack anything that moves, usually bigger than themselves, and then run screaming back to mum when things don't quite work out. I usually keep them on their leads, for their own good.

In the house, it is impossible to keep the place perfectly tidy. At one time if visitors arrived I would run round moving water bowls and dog beds. Now I don't bother. The house is the dogs' home too and people have to accept that. I remember once some people came from a glossy magazine to photograph my house. I was very reluctant for them to do so because it meant disturbing all the animals but in the end I agreed. But how I was to regret it when they arrived. They were so snooty about things. They'd just come from photographing Mike and Bernie Winters' homes. They were lovely, they said, so elegant. It was obvious they didn't see mine in the same category at all.

"It's rather small," they said, looking round my room cluttered with books and pictures. "Very bad to photograph."

Chips looked up from his bed at that moment. I could see the disdain in his eyes. "I'm not moving again, for you or anybody," his look seemed to say. I was inclined to agree with him. The magazine people were so supercilious about the whole thing, I made it a rule that the media don't photograph my home. Damn it, I live here and the dogs do too.

Then there are the birds. I wanted, quite simply, two cockateels and two parakeets. I ended up with thirty-six finches, a canary bought because it looked lonely and finally, and most recently, a single parakeet, also very lonely. Some well-meaning friends bought me two African finches in a tiny cage. I couldn't bear to see them cramped up so I bought a much bigger cage and four more birds, two cocks and two hens.

Then I had to go away for a while. When I returned I looked in the cage – and then looked again. There were six cocks. I knew they hadn't been there when I went away. Apparently, someone had left the cage open, the birds had got away and in buying replacement birds, he or she couldn't tell the boys from the girls. And presumably thought I couldn't either! So then I had to buy six hens to even things out. And, of course, as families do, they multiplied several times. Cages were abandoned long ago. Their aviary now spreads almost the width of the house.

The arrival in the house of Fred the parakeet came as a surprise even to me. And I was the one who bought him. I went into the pet shop to buy fish food – and came out with a young parakeet. I saw him sitting there in his cage, all alone and looking rather dejected. I'd no intention of buying any more creatures. Certainly not another bird. But I had to buy him. He's very young and slowly getting to know us. The local bookmaker has one and apparently the bird walks up and down the counter all day. He never tries to fly away. The bookmaker only has to say: "Eh, you. Come on," and the bird goes back to his cage. Almost like a dog. I'm hoping Fred's going to be like that one day.

Fred's developed into a rather independent little fellow. The other day my great friend, Brian Rawlinson, was asking about the animals. "Have you got anything new in the way of livestock?" he said.

"Yes," I replied. "I've got a free-flying parakeet. I was thinking of calling him Arquemond."

"Oh," said Brian. "What a lovely Egyptian name."

"No, no. As in 'Ah come on Fred'," I said.

I have a racehorse too, called Lymond and trained by Nigel

Tinkler. This year, to Tony's and my great delight, he won his first race. Now Lymond is a high-faluting, temperamental gentleman. He certainly needs talking to – yes it's true, I talk to horses. On the day of the race he was beautifully fit, but slightly down. I could tell by the look in his eye.

So, after telling him he was beautiful, marvellous, handsome . . . I then promised to marry him. He certainly cheered up immensely after that and I'm sure it contributed to his winning the race. He won by three lengths but most of the time he was ten lengths ahead of the field. It was the most exhilarating experience I've ever had in my life. He was so proud of himself when he walked into that winner's enclosure – don't tell me that horses don't know. They do. The horse that had gone out nervous, came back high-stepping and very confident. I don't know about keeping that promise to marry him though . . .

This summer I joined the select rank of people, including the Queen and the Queen Mother, who have races named after them. Lord Ronaldshay, of the racecourse executive at Redcar, invited me and I was more than willing to accept. It's a flat race, The Pat Phoenix Stakes, and I hope to see many of you there for the second one next year, cheering on the winners with me.

Tony introduced me to the fun of the races. I love joining in the excitement and perhaps having a very small flutter. But while I'm jumping up and down with the thrill of the race, the other half of me is peeking through fingertips, not daring to watch in case a horse or jockey gets hurt. Tony loves horses and he isn't a gambler by any means. Nor was my mother. But, typically Irish, she was a racing addict and knew the horses. She used to pick a winner every day and occasionally put on sixpence each way.

When I became a little more affluent on *Coronation Street*, earning all of £50 a week in the beginning, I sometimes left her a fiver or a tenner as I went off to work. "Go on, have a go. You always win," I'd say.

It went on for weeks and then one day I came home and said: "You must have had a terrific win today."

"Oh, I did. I did."

"So where's the brass? You can take me out for a drink," I said.

"Oh, no. I only ever put a shilling on each way," she said. "I wouldn't win if I put on any more."

There's me thinking she must be amassing a fortune with all the winners she was getting.

Chapter Fifteen

My mother had a very sad life although she never let it show. She was always brave, outgoing and very protective towards her child. In effect, I was a single-parent child because it was only through my mother's efforts that I managed to survive. I think if my stepfather had had his way I would have been stuck in an orphanage somewhere because there was great hatred between us.

I witnessed drink there for the first time. He was a heavy drinker. We never had any money because when he was working most of his money went on booze. I used to wake in the night and see my mother at the window crying because my stepfather hadn't come home. I vowed at that time that marriage wasn't for me, nor children because it seemed they upset marriages. When I was a little older I asked my mother why there had never been any more children.

"If there had been, you'd have gone to the wall," she said.

My mother was a wonderful person. Everything she did was courageous. She bore it all, the disgrace, as it was then, of my father, poverty, whatever, without crying about it too much. And when she cried, she cried in the night. Perhaps because of her I have always thought it bad manners to cry in public. Even when my mother died, something within me held back the tears. It was six months before I found the release.

Whenever I had gone away I would phone home to tell my mother I was safe and not to worry. So when I arrived, very tired, somewhere in Scotland for an engagement, I went to the telephone and had halfway dialled my mother's number when I remembered she'd been dead six months. And then I cried.

She was some lady; spirited is not the word. In those days when she discovered my father had bigamously married her, that was a terrible slur on a good Irish girl. You can imagine the shame and degradation she must have felt. He had been married to her for sixteen years and all the time had another wife whom he kept too. She did not, like some ladies today, ask for support, alimony, whatever. She took me by the hand, picked up her few simple belongings and left the home as it stood, slamming the door behind her. We went to stay with friends. Not content with working as a char in the mornings, she worked as a mannequin at night to earn some sort of living for us.

That experience gave her so much understanding and sympathy. I remember many years ago, when I was still a child, there was a young girl who lived at the back of us who became pregnant but was unmarried. Now this was at the time when all the lasses were going out with the Yanks. With true British hypocrisy no one said anything until a girl got into trouble and then, my God, the whole thing was suddenly disgusting. Having a baby in those days – and remember there were no pills or anything like that then – was terrible.

This young girl came in for all the gossip of the neighbourhood, including my stepfather. I remember his crude remarks. "I see she's got herself in t'pudding club." My mother raged at him. She took that girl to her side, gave her things which she could hardly spare herself, and told her not to be ashamed. Some lady!

And I reckon, in a smaller way, so is Elsie Tanner. In so many ways there is a lot of my mother in Elsie – the kind, understanding bit. When the newspapers were making such a fuss over the Mike and Deirdre affair in the Street, reporters rang me to ask what Elsie Tanner thought of it. According to the script she knew nothing about it then, and I was annoyed they had nothing better to write about. But they were insistent. What would Elsie say?

"She'd say mind your own bloody business," I told them, "as she's had too much trouble caused in her own life by gossips."

That was surely my mother speaking through Mrs Tanner. And like my mother Elsie is scrupulously honest. Oh yes, she'd lie for her mates without even thinking twice, but about herself, never. If you said to Elsie: "By God, you're not wearing well," she'd say: "I know. Look at the bloody lines."

Elsie is the big earth-mother figure of the Street. In her way, my mother was too. She mothered everybody and everything. I remember her cutting the corns off a hen and bandaging its feet. She got it right, she did. Our home was a haven for every waif and stray – cats, dogs, kids. She always had something for the kids out of the pantry, even when she hadn't got enough for herself. She would say to people: "You're a damn fool. A fool to yourself," all the while helping them in some way.

Memories of my mother I use in my portrayal of Elsie Tanner. Her funny sayings, her pride, her wisdom. She is around me even now more than anyone or anything else. In times of desperation the cry is still, "Oh mum." I don't think you ever grow out of that.

Of course, we had tremendous rows, veritable fireworks. Two Irish tempers going at the same time, can you imagine? I used to say she was an emotional blackmailer, and so she was. She knew damn well she could never force me to do anything. But if she said: "I'm terribly disappointed in you. You've hurt my feelings" – oh, blimey. I'd do anything for her if she cried.

But when relations told her she was ridiculous to allow me

to go into the theatre, that there was no money to be made and why didn't I get a sensible job, she stood by me stoically. She used to say: "Do what you want but don't hurt yourself. And the way you'll hurt yourself is by hurting someone else."

Years later her belief in me, her pride, shone strongly on her face whenever she came with me on any public appearance. Yes, she was Elsie Tanner's mother and I was more proud of her than of my own achievement.

Every morning I wake, get out of bed, stretch and say my little prayer:

> "Infinite spirit, thy will be done.
> Today is a perfect day,
> I give thanks for that perfect day.
> Today is a day of completion,
> I shall see miracle after miracle,
> And wonders shall never cease."

And, you know I do. I really do. Take one day recently. On the way out I saw a small flower pushing its way through the still-cold earth. A tiny splash of colour when I wouldn't have expected it. A goldfinch settled on a bush as I got into the car. In the studios I managed to get through my lines – there were quite a lot of them – without too much bother. That was a miracle in itself. I received a small orchid. A pretty pink orchid from Cheryl Murray to say thanks for a favour. I was given a box of sweet-smelling soaps, three lighters and eighty cigarettes. When I got home the fire was warm and inviting, Kitty and Nell chatting cheerfully in the kitchen, Tony was happy with his day's work and Fred the parakeet was cackling with glee. Now that, for one day, ain't bad going.

Seeing something good in the blackest of days is a lesson I learned long ago. In my first book, *All My Burning Bridges*, I wrote about my barmy suicide attempt when I was an out-of-work actress living in a grotty flat in London's Finsbury Park. Madam – me, myself – decided to shuffle off this mortal coil and couldn't even do that properly because the money for the gas meter ran out.

I well remember the blackness, the despair, the sense of failure I felt at that time. Failure in both fields, the emotional and the professional, mattered to me deeply. People everywhere must have experienced those kind of moments. When they last more than half a day they become something terribly frightening. Some people don't have second chances as I did.

I remember the way I was able to look at life with new eyes when I awoke from my miasmic sleep that day. I looked out of the window and where before I had seen only shabbiness and the deserted railway sidings, I saw a tree. It was growing up straight and tall and the wind was blowing through its branches. It was almost as if it were dancing on top of that heap of rubbish. As I watched it I thought: "That's me. I can be like that tree."

I knew then that my attempt at suicide was never meant to be successful. I had to pull out of that blackness. There were still thousands of people out there I had to entertain. People I had to show the way to, when I didn't know it myself very well. There were a lot of roles I had to play for a lot of people. I didn't know it then, of course. Now I know I have a function, obscure though it may be. I enjoy giving pleasure. I enjoy seeing a slow smile start on someone's face and spread into a grin.

Sometimes, being entertainers, we are able to help people in many little ways. So many people out there are asking to be helped. Some I can help. A hundred others I can't. People sometimes put too much faith in me. I'm capable of making the most terrible mistakes. They're mistakes of the heart, not criminal ones. I think people can recognise a born lunatic when they see one.

If you're on the television long enough and you're not hiding behind a caricature or a heavy disguise, where the real you is completely hidden, I think your own personality comes through – warts and all. There are certain people on television the public hate and no amount of saying they're not really like that will change people's minds. On the other hand, you could attribute that to their being extremely good actors.

Being an emotional person, the things that have happened in my life – my 'accident of birth', my stepfather, being without money, without work, without love – were the most difficult to ride. I'm not saying my heart was broken, but it was badly cracked a few times. I had to carry my head high on very many occasions when my feet were dragging the dirt. There were people who tried to help. I remember Arthur Dooley, the Liverpool docker who was to become a famous sculptor, introducing me to Father Charlie Lynch.

There was a character. Father Lynch was at one time Information Officer for the Catholic Church in Liverpool and is now a parish priest in the city. Apart from his marvellous pastoral work he has two very unusual claims to fame. On one brief occasion he acted as unofficial press officer for Tracy Austin, the young American tennis star, and on another he sang – hymns, of course – with Bing Crosby. He met both on his regular exchange visits to America.

We used to talk long into the night about religion and faith and he was terribly helpful when I was having problems with Alan. I once did a little job for Father Charlie, opening a jumble sale or something. When I got to the hall I saw lots of women helping, doing odd jobs, preparing for the event. They told me that locally they were nicknamed Charlie's Angels. Well, I'm one of Charlie's Angels too, but I'm the one with the dirty face.

I'm the original cock-eyed optimist. Tony thinks I'm retarded, that I finished growing up at fourteen. He's quite right. I still have my childlike dreams. People as they get older forget how to dream. They rely more on memory. But if you are still capable of building a dream, I believe you can make dreams come true. That way you'll stay young for ever. I became an actress because at some time, a long, long way back, so far back I can't remember when, I said to myself: "I am going to become a famous actress." I didn't know I was going to become infamous. I made my dream.

I am growing older. Of course I am. And I don't enjoy seeing each fresh wrinkle or feel a joint get stiffer. But, God knows, I'm a trier. I've reached this age and I'm still in the game. I've not resigned myself to the bad back and the slightly cracking bones – and don't intend to.

God grant me grace to face each day with hope,
Each misfortune with courage.
And Lord grant me laughter – the ammunition to fight back.

There are people who believe I'm loaded, that I have money and jewels galore and live in a mansion. If only . . . The fact is I'm trying to keep my head above water just like everybody else these days.

I'm absolutely daft with money. I still can't work out the value of things in 'new' money – well, it's still new to me even after all these years of decimal currency. Tony tries to explain the price in terms of 'old' money. "Do you realise that thing cost nearly seven and six?"

"What!" I say in horror and disbelief. "Is that how much 36p really is?" But it's too late. I've bought the damn thing by then.

Perhaps one of the few sensible things I've ever done where money is concerned, is buy my own house. Even then it's not exactly a Hollywood mansion. More a mad house. It's un-assuming and cluttered – a comfortable disorder I say, downright untidy say others – with books, paintings and pretty things I've collected over the years. I like it like that.

There's one great benefit in the way my house looks from outside. Fans don't think I could possibly live there. They're always knocking on the door of the large, grand house next door asking for Elsie. The truth is I don't measure up in many ways to the image fans have created for me, of the big 'star' living it up every night. I've got simple tastes and I really don't enjoy big soirées. I'd rather curl up in front of the fire when I get home, with a good book or talk with Tony, watch the television or listen to music. Elsie Tanner may knock back the gin and tonic but Pat Phoenix drinks very little. And she hates G and T!

I seldom go to nightclubs, but I do go, when I can, to a health club in Manchester to swim in peace. It's the only exercise I get – with all the dashing about I do it's probably all I need. I enjoy going to the opera but it's just as nice to listen to the music I love at home. When I was on my own my music was a great source of comfort. I could listen to it whenever I wanted – four o'clock in the morning if the fancy took me – because there was no one else to worry about. But it has to be real music – opera, classical music, brass bands I love. Pop music I loathe.

How I came to write a pop song I'll never understand. Tony was the manager of a band called Putsch and was writing songs for them. One in particular, 'Solidarity', about the struggles in Poland he wrote with much care, love and feeling. It was going to be recorded but he needed a flip side.

"What can you do?" he asked me. I write poetry and had written a couple of songs before so he knew I could come up with something. "Make it a simple beat."

"I don't know anything about pop music or beat. All I can give you are the words," I said. I wanted to write something about the way this beautiful planet of ours is being destroyed by man's own greed – war, disaster and world pollution. All I could think of was the Four Horsemen of the Apocalypse.

The record was released and 'The Four Horsemen' was played constantly for a time in Madrid, of all places. The kids were listening more to the music, I'm sure, than the words.

Some dizzy reporter asked me at the launch of the record, "Who are these four horsemen, anyway?"

"They're Plague, Pestilence, Famine and Death. And they're riding this earth even now," I said, leaving one still mystified reporter behind.

This year on St Valentine's Day the song was re-released and taken up by CND as their theme song. The record didn't cost a lot to make, yet it had quite an effect on certain people. The best things don't have to cost the earth. I'm a great believer in make do and mend.

I remember not too long ago I was asked to go to a very posh do at the races. One of those times when a lady has to wear a hat – and a stunning one at that. I had plenty of hats but none that would fit the bill. But I was determined not to buy one that would probably be worn just that once. Have you seen the price of fancy hats these days? So I took a very old, plain pill-box hat and dressed it up with feathers from my bit box. Actually, it was a stuffed bird, something I would never buy these days but it was so old, Victorian I think, and therefore excusable I hope. The finished hat looked superb and the newspapers had a field day with pictures of me in my extravagant hat. It had cost absolutely nothing!

I get people writing to me asking where did I get the wonderful evening dress I wore on television the night before or the suit Elsie wore last week. The truth is so often disappointing. Some of my clothes are very old, things I have kept from the last time they were fashionable, some of them have been passed on by friends who have outgrown them, others are from second-hand shops.

Poverty is so bloody humiliating, something that no one should have to endure. I know, because I've been through it and so has Tony. Not having enough to eat, not having the money to stay somewhere, but never borrowing. My mother would never borrow. She'd pawn her wedding ring before that. I've been down to that last-pair-of-stockings situation where the one pair is shared between flatmates. Whoever had the audition that day got to wear the stockings.

So it is unthinkable to me to spend £300, £500 or even more on an evening dress I can wear on public appearances at most twice. Instead, I haunt the second-hand shops and when I've worn something a couple of times I take it back and swop it for something else. In that sense, no I'm not rich, but in another I am. I have a life that is injected now with humour and I enjoy the simple pleasures of life. I never, even during the worst times, stopped seeing beauty around me. The sad part about it was that the beauty I saw was only for me; I had no one to share it with.

Tony and I discovered that we have so much in common in spirit. We share many of the same likes and dislikes. During those deep discussions by the fire which carried on long into the night we realised we were two halves making a whole. We argue – of course we do. We have the mother and father of rows but they never seem quite real. Most of it is to do with me being quite contrary. If Tony has rigid views on one thing, I feel bound to have opposing views. After all – I'm Irish.

Chapter Sixteen

Situation comedy writers are always looking for laughs. They want to be with me sometimes when I meet members of the public. Some of the things they say are hilarious. Their patter, often unwittingly and in all innocence, is better than some of the comedy shows we see on television.

During our summer season last year in Eastbourne, Tony and I took the chance to do all the tourist things, walking down the pier or along the prom on sunny days, whatever took our fancy. After a while I realised our walkabouts were causing some consternation among the holidaymakers. They suddenly discovered we were there. On one occasion a voice rang out: "Eee, it's 'er, with 'im. And they're walkin' about!"

Quite what they expected us to do I'm not sure. Perhaps go about on wheels. Whatever, it was quite unsettling.

I used to tell funny stories on stage every night about what people had said during the day.

"She's not as fat as she is on telly, is she Arthur?"

"Oh, she doesn't look half as old in real life, does she?"

"She's looking a bit off, isn't she? Is she poorly?"

"Ooo, but she's looking marvellous, isn't she? For her age, I mean."

One thing about crowds is that they speak about you as if you're not there. Usually it's right in your ear. I can't have any illusions about myself by the time they've finished with me.

They want to know why I don't do this or that on the Street, forgetting I'm at the mercy of the scriptwriters. They're always pleased when I get a big row scene. The public, it appears, love me to lose my temper. The fiery redhead bit. Proving, I suppose, that there's life in the old girl yet.

Any change in my appearance is a topic of conversation with the public. They would like me to stay the same way forever. In the early days I was overweight – still am for that matter – and lined up to play Mrs Tanner. I was too young for the part but I had put on a lot of weight while I was out of work. An enormous amount in fact. I went up to eleven stone. Rather disgusting, because my average weight is between nine stone and nine stone six. Anyway, what matter? It helped me to get the part. The extra weight, the French pleat they made me put my hair in and a few skilfully applied lines on my face, and I looked the age the script demanded for Elsie. After a few years when the character was well established – and I had a few lines of my own on my face – I was able to do without the heavy make-up and I secretly slimmed and lost a great deal of weight.

The television cameras do make people look heavier than they really are, about ten pounds heavier. Add to that the fact that before I do a play in the theatre I always slim and you can see why some people get a little confused. One in particular I'll always remember. I was on tour and was asked to appear at some function. A little fella came up to me, fighting through the crowd up to the counter behind which I was sitting. He wore a flat cap, had no bottom teeth and was so small his nose barely reached the top of the counter.

"I've gone right off thee," he said.

"Why?" I asked, wondering what I could possibly have done.

"Eee, nay. On t'screen you're a lovely big bausant bugger. In real life, eee, thay's nowt a pound."

He was obviously very disappointed. Perhaps he had always thought I was some six foot, fifteen stone lady.

Colour television, too, brought its disappointment for some viewers. It's difficult to remember in these days of high technology and colour tellies in almost every home, that when *Coronation Street* first started, and for a long time after, all televisions were black and white. No one saw Ena Sharples or Annie Walker or Elsie Tanner in colour. Viewers had to use their imagination – and use it they did. Many had a certain picture of me in their minds which was shattered with the coming of colour to the screen. Suddenly the world found out I was a redhead with green eyes. The consternation when they discovered I wasn't the dark-haired, dark-eyed, tempestuous creature they thought I was. You can imagine my mail.

Some letters accused me. "You were never a redhead before." It was ridiculous. I've been a redhead all my life except for the time a theatre management made me go blonde and my hair fell out.

The early years in the theatre were more than good training. They left repertory actresses and actors with a vast range of experience to draw on. Some young members of *Coronation Street* aren't so lucky. They are suddenly and sometimes unexpectedly thrown into fame. The first hard fact they have to face is that they can no longer behave as they did before. They become popular public figures and the eye of the world – and its press – is upon them.

There are definite rules of Do Not Ever:

Do not ever get drunk in public.

Do not ever be caught canoodling in the back of a car.

Do not ever, as I have learned to my cost, state your own, personal opinion forcibly about this, that or t'other. You're bound to be pilloried for it.

Most important of all, do not ever argue in public.

Tony and I had one of our funniest rows in the supermarket.

I'm a great dasher arounder. I dart frantically about, throwing great masses of things into shopping baskets. Tony is a much more careful shopper. After all, years of frugality and trying to make ends meet when the elastic didn't stretch that far makes him much more discerning.

On this particular day I was shopping for a whole month. It must have appeared to Tony like I was shopping for a siege. Chances to go shopping don't come very often for me, I'm usually so very busy. So large amounts of dog meat, teabags – mountains of 'em 'cause we use that many – masses of butter, biscuits, God knows, the lot, were piling up in the trolley.

I could see Tony's face go a little white. Finally he was forced into protest. "What on earth do you want all that for?" he asked.

"Well, you see . . . " I said. I didn't get any further. He proceeded to tell me off in the middle of the supermarket for what he saw as my extravagance. As fast as I was putting things in the trolley, he was pulling them out.

"You don't want that, for starters. And what are you going to use that for?" he asked.

It developed into a row. I sprang to my defence and the row got louder and louder. I suddenly turned and noticed half a dozen people nearby had stopped what they were doing and were all very intent on hearing what we were saying.

I glared at Tony and said, sotto voce: "If you must row with me in public, will you kindly hiss in future." The row dissolved into laughter. Since then Tony has been known in this household as Hissing Sid.

So you don't always remember the rules. Often you react on pure instinct. Like the night, very late, when we walked into a hotel in a town somewhere. We were stopping there the night before going on to another function. There was a whole crowd of rather smashing young men. CND supporters. The lounge was full of them.

"Hey, Elsie!" A great cry went up as I walked in. "Elsie, come over. Come and see us." I left my friends at the reception desk and went round to say hello to the boys. They were all very nice, pleased to see me.

One young man – who was probably do or daring – was stood behind me. And he dared. He actually dared. He put his hand on my leg under my skirt. I think what he was trying to do was be very clever. To miss actually touching me by a hair's breadth. But he didn't. His hand was actually on my leg.

Now he was behind me and I never looked round. I landed out with an enormous backhander. Instant territory rights. Thump. My hand shot out and cracked him one across the face. I hit the right target – more by luck than anything else. In a crowd I could have hit anybody. He stood there, shell shocked and speechless.

"How dare you," I spluttered. "How dare you do that. How . . . Do you realise I'm old enough to be your . . . er, your mother?"

One of the lads said, very sheepishly: "Yes. But you don't look it, Miss Phoenix."

The young man was absolutely distraught and the others were upset too. They sent me a bottle of champagne to apologise later that night. I really think it was a bit of the daring that made him do it. The poor lad got in terrible trouble from the rest of them, I think. I remember his pale, startled face, standing there saying over and over again in disbelief, "She hit me. She hit me."

People recognise the face. They don't always remember the name. I was opening a fête in some northern town a long way from home. The mayor got up on the platform to give his introductory speech. "Ladies and gentlemen. It is, um, a great pleasure this afternoon to 'ave with us our favourite celebrity. A most famous lady. A lady that has been with us for many years. A lady that needs no introduction. You all know her name. May I welcome to you . . . Mrs . . . er, Miss . . . um . . . (little fumbling with the notes), er, Elsie Phoenix."

What could I do? I got up, smiled broadly to the crowd and said: "Well, this is Elsie Phoenix speaking."

People frequently misspell my name. Feenix or Phenonix even Fenicks. I get all sorts of versions. But I have never, ever regretted taking the name. I'm still very much the Phoenix. I do not know how many times the mythical bird renews itself, rising again out of its own ashes, out of its flames, but I seem to be doing it regularly – twice a year.

I'm not the only one who suffers from misspelled names, mistaken identity. Recently, Tony and I went to a premiere in Manchester. *The Boys In Blue* it was, the Cannon and Ball film. Now I'm rather fond of the Chief Constable of Manchester, James Anderton. He's a handsome, smashing family man with a good humoured twinkle in his eye. On this particular night he and his wife were sitting behind us. When the show was over we turned to talk to them. A lady journalist Tony knows slightly, staggered up. "Who's he?" she asked in her rich ginny voice, pointing at the Chief Constable.

"He's one of the boys in blue," Tony said.

"Oh. Bleedin' actor, is he?" she said.

"No, actually," said Tony, "he's — "

She didn't give him a chance to finish. "Look, love," she said, "you must know all the places round here. You know I like poker. There must be an illegal poker game going on somewhere."

The Chief Constable was spluttering with laughter beside us.

"Why don't you ask him?" Tony said turning to James Anderton.

"Why, would he know?" the journalist said.

"Oh, yes. He'd know."

She turned to the Chief Constable. "Well, would you know,

darling, where there's a poker game going on?"

"I used to," he said, his face stern but eyes twinkling. "Until I closed them all down."

"Yes," said Tony. "He's also noted for closing down the best little whorehouse in town."

"Blimey. I don't believe it," the lady journalist said. "You really are one of them. A copper," she gasped.

Letters we receive by the sackload. Some loving, some begging and a very few, I'm glad to say, nasty. Quite often they contain the strangest things. One recent week's mail of mine, for example, contained, apart from letters, two old copies of a magazine, a newspaper, four hand-made plastic rain hats (I've had about twenty-two of those altogether from the same old man) and a second-hand gabardine sent without a postage stamp.

Julie Goodyear and I have decided we're going to compile a book of some of the oddest letters we've received. Should be good for a laugh. But some of them make you cry.

We care about our fans. We have the regulars who have been writing to us for years. One lady who had been writing to me for at least fifteen years – and I to her – recently passed away. I met her at a function. She suffered from arthritis and was in a wheelchair but got her daughter to take her to the shop where I was appearing, struggling to push the chair through the crowds.

We were introduced and on impulse I gave her a piece of china as a memento. After that she wrote regularly, always starting her letters, "My queen . . . " Her daughter wrote to me when she died. "My mother was happy to the end. Your letters kept her cheerful."

There was also the couple who came to see me when I was doing *The Miracle Worker* on tour. The husband wrote to me first to ask could they see me after the show. "My wife has been in a mental home for many years. She is a great fan of yours and it is only because you are appearing in the theatre that she has been allowed out for the evening," he wrote. I don't think they managed to see the play but they did come round to my dressing room afterwards. A lovely couple.

They brought me a Victorian lady's silver watch. "It's the only thing we've ever had of any value. This visit means so much to us, we'd like you to have it," they said. I was overwhelmed, touched and slightly embarrassed. A gift like that I couldn't refuse. We struck up a correspondence and I still write to them about once a month. Her husband writes regularly – chatty letters, telling me how she is and how he's coping – and I'm extremely fond of both of them. The watch is still with me. It keeps good time and I wouldn't part with it for the world.

Some of the letters I get are very badly written, barely legible. It used to be a source of some amusement amongst the cast of *Coronation Street* to see who had the most illiterate mail. But then you learn that the writer is crippled or has arthritis or is dyslexic. So I don't laugh now. I read them all and where I can, I help. There is one lady who has been a fan of mine for years. She has no one, other than her cat, and is desperately lonely. Nell sees her quite a lot for me and has arranged for someone to call at the house regularly to make sure the lady gets proper meals.

They're not fans any more. They become my personal concern. After years of writing to me I know their problems and their case histories. Like my dancer friend who writes regularly. I found out she had a couple of leg operations and will never dance again. It's a tragedy she tries to hide in her chatty letters.

I admit I loathe writing letters and I'm inundated with them every day. I ought to think myself lucky. Some people wait all year round and never get a letter. However they're addressed,

they usually find their way to me. The postmen cope marvellously. Some are simply addressed to 'Elsie Tanner, Coronation Street', or 'Pat Phoenix, somewhere in Cheshire'. They all
land on my desk eventually.

Not all of them are tragic. During a short spell out of
Coronation Street this year because of back trouble, I got a card
from some university students which made me smile. It was
addressed to Patricia Phoenix and asked me to send their best
wishes to "your friend Elsie Tanner". I wrote back saying
"my friend Elsie Tanner" thanked them for their concern.

I get begging letters too, some of them from charities. If I
gave to every charity that asked me to send something personal for their auction or jumble sale, I wouldn't have a stick of
furniture or a rag to stand up in. I get, on average, about twelve
of those every week. I do support certain charities though.
There's animals of course, and old people. Everyone thinks of
the children but rarely of the aged.

Chapter Seventeen

As I write this Tony and I are planning our summer season in Bournemouth. As you read this, the final curtain will have fallen, the props packed away and the summer crowds returned home.

The summer goes so quickly but at this stage we are caught up in that sense of excitement that goes with each new production. Will it go well? Will the visitors enjoy it? It's always the same. That first week of rehearsal both of us say, "Oh, I'm never going to get this character. I don't know. What am I doing this for?"

An actor can read a part on a superficial level. What is important to Tony and me is that we become the people we play. When it comes right it's like the turning on of an electric light switch. I always call it the click. If I don't get it, to me the part I'm playing is never satisfactory. Sometimes the click can come on stage. Bedonk! You've suddenly got it. Instant takeover – you become that other person. It's exciting when it happens. Terribly exciting. You are host to another individual.

I have eerie memories of it happening on stage when I was playing Blanche Dubois in *A Streetcar Named Desire*. I was very young, much too young for the part, really. But the management wanted me to play it and I wanted to play it too. I'd been rehearsing all week and I wasn't sure I'd got her. I was weighing in at seven stone – I'd lost pounds just rehearsing. To learn that show in a week while you're playing another one is some marathon. It's such a heavy, emotional play. It rips you to pieces. I played it not only once but a dozen times throughout my career and each time, as soon as I started to rehearse, I dropped weight. I could go in at ten stone and be down to seven every time I played it.

I was terribly nervous on this particular night, I remember. It was Halifax and the theatre was packed. I heard their muffled voices and was a mass of nerves as I waited to go on. I remember Douglas Young, who was playing Stanley, standing beside me, trying to tell me a joke to take my mind off things. I didn't want that. I wanted to be Blanche. I heard the jangled music of the Vesuviana and wandered on in a daze.

"They had told me to take a streetcar named Desire. Transfer to one called Cemetery and get off at Elysian Fields," – I said Blanche's first lines . . . and I remember no more. I remember nothing. There are eight scenes in *Streetcar* and I have no recollection of doing that show until I was stood at the footlights at the end. Someone was saying: "Another bow. Another bow." It was a standing ovation. It came to me very far away. Very, very far away because I was still hearing the music. "Da, de, da, de, da. Da, de, di, de, di." It was the weirdest experience – the most wonderful experience. But agonising.

The summer season this year pleases us both very much because we're re-opening a theatre. It's a small, beautiful theatre that's been used for a long time now as a bingo hall. I think it's very sad the way so many theatres are forced to close these days. Sad but perhaps understandable with the tax and VAT they have to pay.

Long before my time there were fifty-two theatres in Manchester. A company could come to the city and play a whole year with the same show, going from theatre to theatre. Each place had its own following. Even in my time there were at least nine theatres left. Now there is the one major one and a couple of smaller places.

In those days everyone went to the theatre at least once a week. My parents went as often as they could, taking me with them. My father should have been in the theatre – he was a thwarted song-and-dance man. My earliest recollection is as a babe-in-arms in the theatre. They would stick a dummy in my mouth and take me to watch the young George Formby. But these days the price of seats in the big theatres is ridiculous. What ordinary working man, or unemployed person for that matter, can afford tickets? There is still a lot of good value in the theatre today, for all that, and much of it is coming from outside London. From places like Liverpool.

In Bournemouth, Tony and I are playing continentals in Agatha Christie's *The Verdict*. We're both going round with faintly foreign-sounding accents. Ernst Walder, who's coming along to understudy, has no need to practise the voice. He's got it already. Brian Rawlinson, a friend and my favourite director in the theatre, is directing this one as he did last year's summer season.

Once the first, difficult week is over, it's great fun. We have a constant stream of visitors to stay – Nell, Kitty, Carole, Keith, all the gang. For me it's as good as a holiday, getting out into the theatre for a while. It's compulsive with me. I have to get back into the theatre. I love it.

I'm not the world's greatest organiser and I have to admit I am very untidy. I'm always in a rush. You know, straight through the door, dropping coats, bags and books in the middle of the floor as I go. But somehow I manage to run myself successfully, with a little help from my friends. I may forget to write down dates and details of what I'm supposed to be doing but it's stored in my brain somehow and I get there in the end.

I was booked to do a late night show one time and Tony was driving me there. We were well on the road when I said to him: "When we get to Carlisle — "

"What?" said Tony.

"When we get to Carlisle — "

"We're not going to bloody Carlisle. We're going to Cardiff," he said.

We managed to stop the car and get out the papers. And yes, it was Cardiff. I'd just had a mental block about the name of the place but Tony nearly had a fit.

It's not always my fault. Many times people ask me to do things but omit the salient details. For instance, I once arrived at an enormous town hall somewhere in England to do an appearance. In all the excitement they had forgotten to tell me what the appearance was for and I was shunted on to the stage so quickly there was no time to ask. All I could see were fires and papers scattered about the room. Now, how the hell do you open a function when you don't know what it is? I adlibbed one of the most terrific speeches in my career, saying how glad I was to be there, to see so many people and I hope they had an enjoyable afternoon.

" . . . and so I am very pleased to declare this, er, function, well and truly open." I hadn't a clue what it really was. In fact it was a National Coal Board do – hence the fires.

The same thing happened to me at a Sunday-night concert at which I'd agreed to appear for charity. I presumed they just wanted me to go on stage and make a speech on behalf of the charity. I arrived at the theatre to see my name in letters a foot high on the bill with Lance Percival. Inside, the organisers said: "Miss Phoenix, you're doing twenty-five to thirty minutes."

"I'm doing what?" I spluttered.

"Twenty-five to thirty minutes. There's no problem is there?"

"No," I said, blithely.

Now I'm not a variety act, I'm a straight actress. I can keep going for fifteen minutes or so, or give after-dinner speeches, but a concert performance! Luckily I was early. I locked myself in the loo and wrote a comedy script. An hour or so later the act went down very well, more because they loved me, I think, than because the jokes were all that good.

I'm sure things won't be any different in my old age. I can see myself turning out to be a feathery, absent-minded lady, at least as far as the factual things of life are concerned. My mother once said, shortly before she died: "You'll never be grown-up. Not as long as you live." How right she was. I don't particularly want to be if that means removing all the things I believe in. A joy in beauty, loving innocence, wanting the whole world to be free and happy.

With my background I had to be individual, a one-off. My boss once asked, after yet another scrape I'd got myself into: "Why does it always happen to you?"

"How the hell do you expect me to be normal?" I said, "with two crazy but wonderful people like my parents? It's a wonder I'm not in the looney bin!"

I have these crazy ideas. On the spur of the moment and usually at some ridiculous time. "Let's have a picnic," I said one cold February day. Outside the snow lay thick on the ground and the sky was heavy and threatening. "Let's have a picnic."

The whole gang was at my house – including Joe Boyer, then a director on the Street. They looked a bored, miserable lot. No one wanted to do anything.

"Pat," they said, as if talking to a thick child. "It's snowing outside. People don't have picnics in the middle of February."

"We do," I said, my mind made up. "Let's go up and see Wordsworth's cottage in the Lake District."

We ordered two enormous hampers, one full of food, the other full of champagne, and packed them in my car. Eight of us crammed into it including Fred the cat who'd walked in one day and just been accepted as part of the family. The other six squeezed into the second car and we set off in convoy. None of us knew where we were going. Some suggested Bronte land, others wanted to find Wordsworth's cottage.

We drove out into the countryside, all crisp and white around. It was one of those bright, sunny but cold winter's days. We'd gone about thirty-six miles – that's when we suddenly realised the other car wasn't with us. And we had the food and the champagne. Those of us in the first car gleefully drove up to Wuthering Heights. The other car was nowhere in sight. We sat up there on the moor, with the wind howling and a few grey clouds gathering overhead, drinking champagne and congratulating ourselves for the fact that we had the grub and the others were probably hopelessly lost by that time.

At the end of the day – after chasing Fred back into the car – we set off back home. The others had been all day wandering round looking for us without food. We headed for a restaurant that had a swimming pool and saunas. Hopefully, we thought, we might meet up with the others there. We drove into the car park as dusk was falling and there were the others – haggard, pale and palpitating with hunger – waiting for us. They had, of course, gone to find Wordsworth's cottage.

We finally went into the saunas. There was a lot of tiptoeing about. Everyone pinching everyone else's clothes from lockers and hiding them. I got caught, by Joe Boyer, tiptoeing out of the men's changing room with a handful of clothes. He turned and chased me. Fortunately I had a towel wrapped round me. As he chased me I flung the ladle from the sauna at him – with full intent to miss. It didn't. It hit him and knocked him out. There was great consternation. People were pouring out of the saunas from every direction. The single-sex saunas suddenly became mixed. Everybody was grabbing towels, administering first-aid. Absolute chaos. Anyway, all ended well. We all finished up having a party when we got back home.

My friends are used to my mad ideas. It's great fun when you have others with you who also act on impulse.

Chapter Eighteen

People show such interest about Tony's burns. In one way I think it's the strange fixation the British have about operations, hospitals and health. In another, it is genuine concern. Often it comes from the most unlikely quarters and in the most unsubtle ways.

The first time it happened we were at some big soirée, full of respectable, hatty ladies. One of them came up and engaged me in conversation. Tony was about three feet away, talking to someone else.

"What a shame about Mr Booth's burns," she said. "How terrible for him. But they don't really show, do they?"

The conversation progressed to more mundane matters. "These cakes are rather nice, aren't they?" and "Do you rehearse every day in *Coronation Street*?"

Then back to the nitty gritty, the question she'd been dying to ask all evening. "I hesitate to ask this . . . but is Mr Booth, um, Mr Booth . . . (in a rasping whisper) is he all right down there?" Nod, nod.

Tony overheard and burst into a great roar of laughter. I hastened to tell her: "Yes, as far as I know, he's all right there."

That question has been asked, or rather not asked but implied, on so many occasions. And always by the most respectable of ladies. They come up to me mouthing like a Les Dawson character.

"Has it affected him, um, in, you know, that way?"

"Is he, well you know . . . ?"

I suppose I could have let them stew in their own juice and say, no, I didn't know what they meant. But, funny as it always sounds, such concern is usually well meant. In a sense Tony shouldn't have been all right. The shock of burning sometimes continues long after the actual burns have healed. People have been made impotent for life. And Tony was told he would be impotent for two years. But Tony, being Tony, wasn't.

He thinks his scars are terribly noticeable. I don't.

I've only ever seen one woman turn away from them. When we were in Yugoslavia there were two beaches at Sveti Stevan we could use, the private beach for the hotel or the public beach where all the Yugoslavians went. On the hotel beach one day Tony came out of the sea and I saw a woman from the hotel, a tourist, grimace and turn away. I don't know what she thought he'd got.

"Right, we don't come on this beach any more," I told Tony. "We go where the locals are."

They were wonderfully kind and showed great interest in his burns without embarrassment.

Some time before that holiday I hired a local swimming pool to get Tony to swim because he wouldn't go anywhere where he had to show his burns. The pool was closed to outsiders and, in the company of a few friends, he swam for the first time.

In another way I rather threw him in at the deep end, socially at least. Tony wasn't used to being with crowds after his long stay in hospital and the prospect of going out and meeting people again was, to his mind, a daunting one. He felt the world still hated him after the reports of his past. But I was doing public appearances at charity functions and so on, and Tony wanted to be with me.

The first time he accompanied me was on a date when we had to drive down through the town in an open carriage. It was one of the most moving experiences for him since he'd come out of hospital. People came up to him, genuinely glad to see him back in the public eye.

"Good on you, lad. Get better soon."

"Take good care of her, son."

"Be happy, the two of you."

The greetings and good wishes rang out from all sides. It was tremendous. I don't think Tony had seen people react to him like that for a long, long time. They were patting him on the back and on the knee where they couldn't see his burns. Some of it hurt but I don't think he noticed. He was too happy.

He also had to learn what it felt like to be recognised again on the street and not just on public occasions. One winter's day we decided to have an outing to Blackpool.

"Come on," I said. "You haven't been there for years and it'll be great fun. We'll do all the daft touristy things. We'll walk along the sea front, go on the beach, take a ride in a carriage. Come on, let's go."

It was a brisk, bright sunny day when we arrived and although it was out of season we found a carriage. Bowling along, Tony suddenly decided to kiss me. He leaned over and just as he was planting a kiss on my cheek, we turned a corner. There on the street was a great crowd of people who saw him. They burst out cheering.

"Ah, got you."

"Good on you, Tony."

"Great Tony, great Elsie."

We both dissolved into giggles. "I had forgotten that everyone knows you," he said. "And they still remember me."

I suppose I gave him back some sort of faith in people. Up until then he believed luck had run against him, that he wasn't wanted and had been crossed off the list. Seeing the way people rallied round with all the best wishes in the world helped to change all that.

With the old calliope hootin' and a tootin' its traditional farewell and the bucket boards slapping the water in time to the music, the *Mississippi Queen* pulled out of New Orleans and down river. Tony and I were steamboatin'.

It was an opportunity I wouldn't have missed for the world. I'd read the books of Mark Twain as a child and fallen in love with them and the Deep South. Here was my chance to explore it for myself. The holiday – a little over a year ago – was a much needed one for both of us after the tensions of the previous months.

"Let's get away," I said to Tony. "I've got the chance to go to America. Anywhere we want. What do you think."

"Great. But I don't really fancy Florida or any of the usual places," he said.

"Nor do I. But there's a holiday cruise down the Mississippi I've heard about. How about that?"

We flew to New Orleans and spent eight days there altogether and eight days on the paddlewheel steamboat, the *Mississippi Queen*. Eight days just watching that river roll by.

New Orleans was an eye-opener. Tony doesn't drink alcohol at all these days and I'm not a big drinker. But in that town the booze flows night and day if you want it. There's a famous place called Brennan's where for breakfast, starting at 7.30 in the morning, you could have champagne cocktail followed by the most enormous American spread you could imagine. Eggs Benedict, hominy grits, black-eyed peas, grilled steak, french fries, even apple-strudel meringue. And, of course, drinks with everything.

The cruise downriver was sheer heaven, eight days and seven nights aboard the most glorious floating wedding cake.

The boat had everything – swimming pool, cinema, old-fashioned bands in the ballroom, banjo players in the bars and, up on the top deck, the calliope, the steam piano. On a clear day its music could be heard for five miles around. The old tunes, pumped out by Professor Spracklen – 'See them rolling along' and 'All them golden slippers' – brought people running down to the levee to greet the steamboat as she pulled in at the many stops along the way, just as they did a century ago. All around was Mark Twain country.

Houses were kept just as they were in the Civil War days – real Scarlet O'Hara places. Others, newly built, with swimming pools front and back. Everywhere people invited us in, to sit in rocking chairs on porches sipping mint juleps. We travelled through pirate country, past Dead Man's Bend where the bodies of the cut-throats' victims floated down the river. Past Destrehan, the Louisiana plantation where the pirate Jean Lafitte often stayed and where, or so the story goes, his ghost can be seen, walking the levee.

Our guide was a real Southern belle. "Ma name is Mary Lou, and ah'd like to show you Rosedown." The accent seemed almost phoney but it was real Deep South. Her ambition, she said, was to marry a millionaire, live in Britain and appear on television. "Just as, ah believe, you do, Miss Phoenix."

That holiday, for Tony, was when he really began to get back on his feet. The staff on board took great care of him. While I was sipping mint juleps, Tony had milk or special non-alcoholic cocktails they mixed for him. He put on the first weight gain in those lazy, blissful days.

The Mississippi cruise ended with a party night. We watched the river roll by at midnight to the sounds of Dixieland.

The telephone rang in the house one dismal, cold morning

seven months ago. Kitty, who was busy in the kitchen, answered it.

"It's for you," she said to Tony. "It's a fella from the BBC."

Tony took the receiver from her. "Hello, Mr Booth," said the voice on the other end of the line. "It's the BBC's Radio Manchester here. We'd like you to host a new, late-night programme for us."

That was how he came to start his first radio interviewer's job. The show went out every Friday night from ten to midnight, with Tony reading poetry, playing records and interviewing people in the studio. He became so busy we were almost making appointments to see one another. He was always dashing down to the BBC, doing his own research, choosing his music and poetry. I'm always busy too. For a while it seemed we were constantly just missing each other. I even missed his first two shows. I had to be away from home on both nights. On that first Friday I tried to ring him from the hotel where I was staying. I tried the BBC several times but it was late and there was no one on the switchboard. Then I started to ring him at home.

No. He won't be there, I thought, and put down the receiver. He was home. He'd gone straight back after the show. When I got back the next day I asked him how the first night had gone.

"I think I was terrible," he said. He was so nervous about starting a new job.

"I bet you weren't," I said. "I got a friend to tape it. Let's play it back now." Tony left the room very quickly. He didn't want to hear his voice.

I played the tape and thought the show was smashing. Tony has a good late-night voice and the poetry he read was lovely. There was one slight hiccup that first night. Tony wanted to end the show with the record 'Once, Twice, Three Times A

Lady' which he says is his song for me.

"It's nearly midnight and the end of the show," he told listeners. "And to finish we're going to have The Commodores singing 'Once, Twice, Three Times A Lady'. Er . . . no. It's Crystal Gale. No, it isn't. It's The Commodores. No . . . Well, anyway, it's 'Three Times A Lady'."

I knew which song he meant.

Chapter Nineteen

Four be the things I'd been better without;
Love, curiosity, freckles and doubt.

That's Dorothy Parker's view, and she's quite right about three of those things. About the first I've reservations. Love, in many situations certainly, a woman would be better without. At present I can't honestly say that. On the other counts I agree wholeheartedly.

Curiosity? I'm guilty of that in no uncertain way – the most terrible curiosity about everything and everybody. It's got me into more trouble than anything else. Curiosity, it's quite true, surely did kill the cat. One of these days it'll probably kill Pat too.

Freckles? Oh God, freckles all over the place – places that can be seen and some that can't. I've got millions of freckles and I hate 'em. The only time I'm happy is in the summer when they all join up.

Doubt? I've had my share of that too. Even at this late stage of the game I doubt and doubt again, Myself, of course, who else? But in doubting everything, my faith in the infinite spirit never lags. There comes a time in everyone's life when the doubting stops, curiosity diminishes and the freckles don't matter because you've found your alter ego – the love of your life.

And love, in spite of Dorothy Parker's belief, has made Pat Phoenix what she is. Whatever that may be.

It was a very bumpy road we travelled, both Tony and I, to reach these, the last pages. Although an end to this particular story, we hope it's merely a beginning for us. We didn't get here easily. The road for us, as for thousands of other people, has been beset with tears and tragedies. But there have been flowers by the wayside, companionship, compassion and tenderness. It's taken a long time, but we have reached our Dragon Mountain.

Just as the fairy story seems to be coming to an end, and a very grey curtain is about to descend, all of a sudden the third act springs into life. And that can happen to anybody.

Regrets? I can honestly say I don't regret a thing in my life. Every pain, every tear was all part of the learning. All part of the lesson. I wouldn't have had it any other way. I've loved some, hated some. Lost some, won a few. Laughed a lot, cried a lot. Throughout it all wonderment has remained with me. If this book has seemed to you like reading the Perils of Pauline, you ain't seen nothing yet.

All I can say is . . . to be continued.